The Eagle Huntress

The True Story of the Girl Who Soared Beyond Expectations

AISHOLPAN NURGAIV
with LIZ WELCH

LITTLE, BROWN AND COMPANY
New York Boston

Due to language barriers, the authors worked closely with a translator chosen by the family, Yerlan Amankeldi, to ensure that the words in English were the right ones.

Copyright © 2020 by Aisholpan Nurgaiv
Map illustration copyright © 2020 by Virginia Allyn
Discussion Guide copyright © 2020 by Little, Brown and Company

Cover photograph copyright © 2013 by Asher Svidensky. Cover design by Karina Granda. Cover copyright © 2020 by Hachette Book Group, Inc.

Hachette Book Group supports the right to free expression and the value of copyright. The purpose of copyright is to encourage writers and artists to produce the creative works that enrich our culture.

The scanning, uploading, and distribution of this book without permission is a theft of the author's intellectual property. If you would like permission to use material from the book (other than for review purposes), please contact permissions@hbgusa.com. Thank you for your support of the author's rights.

Little, Brown and Company
Hachette Book Group
1290 Avenue of the Americas, New York, NY 10104
Visit us at LBYR.com

First published in hardcover and ebook by Little, Brown and Company in May 2020
First Trade Paperback Edition: June 2021

Little, Brown and Company is a division of Hachette Book Group, Inc. The Little, Brown name and logo are trademarks of Hachette Book Group, Inc.

The publisher is not responsible for websites (or their content) that are not owned by the publisher.

The Library of Congress has cataloged the hardcover edition as follows:
Names: Nurgaiv, Aisholpan, author. | Welch, Liz, 1969– author.
Title: The eagle huntress: the true story of the girl who soared beyond expectations / Aisholpan Nurgaiv with Liz Welch.
Description: New York: Little, Brown and Company, [2020] | Includes bibliographical references. | Audience: Ages 8–12 | Summary: "Eagle huntress Aisholpan Nurgaiv shares her story" —Provided by publisher.
Identifiers: LCCN 2019031299 | ISBN 9780316522618 (hardcover) | ISBN 9780316522601 (ebook) | ISBN 9780316417952
Subjects: LCSH: Aisholpan, Nurgaiv—Juvenile literature. | Falconers—Mongolia—Biography—Juvenile literature. | Girls—Mongolia—Biography—Juvenile literature. | Women hunters—Mongolia—Biography—Juvenile literature. | Falconry—Mongolia—Juvenile literature. | Kazakhs—Mongolia—Social life and customs—Juvenile literature. | Golden eagle—Mongolia—Juvenile literature.
Classification: LCC SK17.A34 A3 2020 | DDC 639/.1092 [B]—dc23
LC record available at https://lccn.loc.gov/2019031299

ISBNs: 978-0-316-52262-5 (pbk.), 978-0-316-52260-1 (ebook)

Printed in the United States of America

LSC-C

Printing 1, 2021

A fast horse and a soaring eagle are the wings of a nomad.

—KAZAKH PROVERB

CONTENTS

PROLOGUE: Seeing My Story for the First Time 1
CHAPTER 1: The White Eagle 11
CHAPTER 2: My People Are Eagle Hunters 24
CHAPTER 3: Nomadic Life 33
CHAPTER 4: A Rite of Passage 49
CHAPTER 5: Tourists 61
CHAPTER 6: Asher Arrives 80
CHAPTER 7: Otto, Not Just Another Excited Tourist 95
CHAPTER 8: How to Train an Eagle 109
CHAPTER 9: Blessings and Opinions 125
CHAPTER 10: The Road to Ölgii 130
CHAPTER 11: The Golden Eagle Festival 139
CHAPTER 12: How to Catch a Fox in the Winter 159
CHAPTER 13: Famous in Mongolia—and Beyond 175
CHAPTER 14: The Aisholpan Effect 188

Acknowledgments 192

Further Reading 195

Kazakh Glossary 196

Discussion Guide 198

About the Authors 200

PROLOGUE

Seeing My Story for the First Time

Nothing was familiar.

It was my second time in the United States and this time it was really hot. I started sweating before we even left the hotel room. The sun beat down in a way that felt totally unfamiliar. In Bayan-Ölgii (pronounced *Ul-ghee*), the northwestern corner of Mongolia where I am from, there's a long, very cold season and then a couple of not-as-cold seasons. Even in our summer, it never gets that hot.

Otto told me I should dress up, so I wore my best outfit: a gray suede embroidered suit that I had bought for special occasions and a white fur hat that I was given as a gift after I won the Golden Eagle Festival back home. Winning was a big deal because I was the first woman ever to win the contest, and at thirteen years old I was the youngest, too.

That was why I was here, in Los Angeles, California, sweating in my gray suede suit.

But I did not care about the heat or the crowd of people surrounding me. I was finally going to see *The Eagle Huntress*, the documentary film that the British director Otto Bell had made about me and my family, and our love of eagle hunting.

I could hardly wait!

Technically, I had seen it when I first came to the United States—that was eight months earlier, back in January, when the film premiered at a festival called Sundance. I was excited and a bit nervous. I did not know what to expect. At least there was snow at Sundance. That felt familiar. Otherwise, my parents and I stood out among the people that swarmed the town. They all had parkas and snow boots and wool hats. They reminded me of the tourists who came to visit us in Bayan-Ölgii. Only this time, we were the tourists.

Two years before, we had never even met Otto, who had traveled to Mongolia to meet me after seeing a photo of me with my brother's eagle. He wanted to make a film about me, he told us, and about eagle hunting. Now here we were, in this foreign country for a second time, because of him.

When we were at Sundance, so many tourists wanted to take a picture of me and my mom and dad, and so many journalists wanted to talk to us that by the time I made it to the theater, I was so overwhelmed and exhausted that I couldn't concentrate on the film! I would not let that happen this time. I knew at last that I would get the chance I had been waiting for since January: to truly see this story that people kept telling me was already inspiring the world. To take in every detail. I had already become famous in Mongolia as the first girl to win this famous contest. But for me, all the attention was still so strange. To have people from such faraway places so interested in my story did not feel real. It was like being in a dream. Everyone in Los Angeles was treating me like a celebrity, which I found so funny!

I am just Aisholpan. A sister, daughter, student, and best friend. A nomadic girl whose happiest moments are still the ones when I'm on my pony, galloping across the steppes of Mongolia. A girl who just wanted to do what boys have always been allowed to do in my culture. I knew in my bones that I could do it better than most—boys or girls.

The crowd at the Hollywood theater was different from the one back at Sundance. The women wore dresses that looked more like underwear, showing so much skin. My mother and I were shocked. The shoes were even more alarming—most of them had heels so high and pointy that I had no idea how these women could stand, let alone walk. The men, however, were mostly in suits, also sweating, like me.

Once again, people shouted my name as I walked down the red carpet with my dad. They wanted photos, so we stopped to let them take a few, but it was so hot and there were so many people that I started to feel dizzy. So I poked my father in his ribs after a few shots and pointed to the theater door. I could not wait to get inside, where it was dark, cool, and quiet.

Otto helped us find our seats, and once the theater was filled, he walked to the front of the room to introduce the film.

I heard him say my name, and the audience clapped. I got up and waved, along with my mom and dad, as Otto introduced them. It was so strange to be surrounded by so many strangers applauding for me. I looked at all these smiling faces, trying to understand why they were so excited to see a film about me. I knew why *I* was excited.

Then the lights dimmed to darkness, and the red velvet curtains parted.

The opening shot made my heart grow big in my chest: It was of the vast desert landscape of the Mongolian steppes, the grasslands interspersed with rocky mountains that I call home. I felt this bursting sense of joy—and longing. Los Angeles felt so foreign to me, with its six-lane highways and mirrored buildings that reflected the sun. And it was so, so far away. Just to be sitting in this seat took four separate airplanes—one from Ölgii, the city closest to my home, to Ulaanbaatar, the capital of Mongolia. Another to Seoul, South Korea, where we flew in at night, when the city looked like a bright, pulsing dream. From there, we flew eighteen hours to New York City. So many tall buildings pierced the sky, earning their nickname "skyscraper." The fourth and final flight brought me here. It took twenty-eight hours in the sky for me to get to this seat in this theater to watch a movie about my life back home.

SEEING MY STORY FOR THE FIRST TIME

What was six PM in Los Angeles was eleven AM the day after tomorrow in Ölgii. Perhaps that was why I felt upside down and inside out. I was lost in time and space, eating strange food and surrounded by funny-sounding and -looking people who all knew who I was. No wonder I felt dizzy.

For centuries, my people, the Kazakhs, have roamed the northwestern corner of Mongolia, where we have been practicing the ancient sport of eagle hunting. It is a sacred part of our culture. I had no idea that it was rare or in threat of extinction. I just knew that I loved doing it, as does my father, as did his father, and his father before him. In my family, eagle hunting goes back seven generations.

Still, seeing the snow-dusted Mongolian steppes fill the screen took my breath away.

When I saw my grandfather appear on the screen, I gasped again. In the film, he is sitting at our family table and we are eating a big plate of noodles and meat. My stomach ached for that very dish, and my heart ached for my grandfather. He had died suddenly six months earlier. Oh, how I wished he could have been in the theater next to me, and not just up on the screen.

In Kazakh culture, eagle hunting is a male rite of passage. Fathers historically teach their sons how to hunt, as my grandfather taught my father. While I have since found out that women hunted in the past, I was the first in my family to do it. When I learned, I did not know another girl who was as keen to become an eagle huntress as I was.

After the film ended, the entire audience leaped to their feet. The applause was so loud, it rippled through my body. I stood up and waved, and may have uttered "*Rakmet*" several times. "Thank you" in Kazakh. All these faces were beaming at me. Some people were even crying, too.

They made me feel like a movie star, just as seeing myself on that big screen had! When Otto Bell had asked if he could make a movie about me, I'd

SEEING MY STORY FOR THE FIRST TIME

said yes because I wanted to share eagle hunting with the world. All I cared about was what that might do for my people, and for other Kazakh girls especially.

Sitting in that theater, as the applause continued to roar around me, I was beginning to understand that this movie I had agreed to participate in had not only documented my life but was changing it as well.

1

The White Eagle

My mother often tells the story of the day before I was born.

"Your grandmother came to visit, and her face was lit up in a way I had not seen before," my mother says. "She had a dream that the White Eagle flew into our house and sat on the perch."

The perch that she is referring to is called a *tughir*. It is more than a century old. It was carved from the roots of a river birch and was handed down from my great-grandfather to my grandfather and finally to my father, who is known as Agilay. It is where all my father's eagles have perched in our home, and his father's eagles had perched in his home before him.

It was also where the real great white eagle—the one my grandmother dreamed about—had once sat.

My father comes from the Tolek tribe of the Kazakh nomads, legendary eagle hunters, who have lived for centuries in Ulaankhus, Mongolia, near a mountain called Khuren Khairkhan, where the great white eagle once soared.

My people, the Kazakhs, are descendants from the Turkik, which means we all speak a similar language and have lived a nomadic life. One theory is that the word *Kazakh* is derived from the Turkish verb *qaz*, which means "to wander." Another theory is that it comes from the Turkik word *quazag*, which means "to gain," as nomads roamed with their herds of animals from one grazing spot to another, trading their animals or products made from them along the way.

THE WHITE EAGLE

Even today, my family lives a seminomadic life, which means that, depending on the season, we move with our animals to bring them to better pastures. Both my parents grew up in nomadic families who lived off the land. Nomads eat what they raise—in our case, goats, cows, and sheep. Not just the meat, but all the things we can make from cows' and goats' milk as well. So we move with our herds, which is why we have moveable homes, which we call *gers*. They are like fortified tents, made of felt and covered in heavy canvas that is wrapped around a wooden structure, which can be easily assembled and disassembled when we move our animals to the next pasture.

Our winter home is permanent, made of wood and plaster, and then lined with animal skins and rugs to keep us warm during the cold Mongolian winters, when temperatures dip to negative sixty degrees Fahrenheit. In the spring, summer, and autumn, we move our herds to different pastures—first over to a valley for the spring, when everything is starting to bloom; then, in the summer, up to the mountains, where the grass is sweet and tender after the snow melts. In these seasonal grazing spots, we erect our gers. Growing up, my father had heard the stories of the White Eagle. All the nomads who lived in the area knew about her. She could catch foxes and baby lambs with great ease and take down big-horned wild sheep in one fell swoop. Someone once witnessed her kill a fully grown wolf, and from then on, her reputation grew.

Legend has it that one day, Dauit—a wealthy nomad who was the governor of that region and had many cows, goats, and even camels, the most expensive animals—made an announcement: "Whoever can catch the White Eagle and bring her to me to hunt with will get a great prize!"

Bulanby was a nomad and one of the best eagle hunters in the region. In Kazakh, we call them *berkutchi*. When he heard of this competition, he decided he would be the one to catch that eagle.

He was not alone.

THE WHITE EAGLE

All the hunters wanted to catch this famed bird and collect the prize. They placed traps and nets throughout the area. But nobody could catch the White Eagle. Except for Bulanby.

He brought the great eagle to Dauit.

Dauit was thrilled. "What is your price?"

Bulanby said, "Train the eagle to hunt for you. I will tell you my price later."

Dauit trained the eagle and went on to catch so many foxes, wild sheep, and even a wolf cub that stories of this great white eagle started to spread beyond Ulaankhus throughout the entire Bayan-Ölgii Province, the area where Kazakh nomads have lived and have hunted with eagles for centuries.

Many months passed, and finally Bulanby returned for his prize.

"You are back, finally!" Dauit said. "What is your asking price for this magnificent bird?"

Bulanby smiled and replied, "Your beloved daughter to marry my younger brother, Bosaga."

After much consideration, and a conversation with his willing daughter, Dauit agreed. When the couple married, Dauit said, "This amazing eagle has the power to feed your family. It is a sign that you will continue the great tradition of eagle hunting for future generations."

Bosaga was my father's great-grandfather.

Dauit's daughter was my father's great-grandmother.

This story is famous in my family, and proof, my dad insists, that we come from one of the greatest eagle-hunting families ever known.

This explains the tears in my grandmother's eyes when she told my mother about her dream. Happy tears, my mother insists.

"It was a good sign," she says.

My mother was looking for them.

After my older brother, Samrakhan—my parents' first child—was born, my mother could not stay pregnant, or "hold" a baby, as she says. She lost four pregnancies, one after another, which is why there is a nine-year age difference between Samrakhan and me.

My parents imagined that they would have a large family, as they live off the land and need many hands to help care for our animals. My father has nine siblings; my mother has eight. They thought their family would be of a similar size.

The first time my mother became pregnant after Samrakhan was born, she lost that baby in the spring.

Spring is the hardest time for nomads—my parents had twenty-five sheep, twenty-five goats, and one cow back then. Spring is when baby animals are born, so at that time my parents hardly slept, as they were always getting up in the middle of the night to check on the pregnant animals.

One night, my mother was awoken by the baying of the cow in distress. My father was gone, likely dealing with other animals. So she quickly got up and ran outside, following the sounds of the crying cow. The moon was bright and cast a silvery glow over the grassland that surrounds our home. She found the cow, on her knees instead of lying down and wailing as if in pain. As my mother came closer, she saw tiny hooves emerging from beneath the struggling cow and started to run toward it. That was when she felt a sharp pain in her own stomach. She ignored it. The mother cow was in trouble, so she grabbed the tiny hooves and tugged. The calf emerged, and as she helped it find its mother to suckle, my mother felt another pain in her own belly.

She was only five months pregnant then, and she believes that the baby was not ready for the world.

After that, each of her three pregnancies ended quickly.

She insists that her womb was still grieving.

So when she got pregnant with me, she went to see a shaman. These are holy men who treat every type of illness—including a grieving womb.

"How can I keep this baby?" she asked.

This shaman was famous in the Bayan-Ölgii Province and beyond. His name was Tserern. He had healed Samrakhan's broken neck the year before, after he was thrown from his horse. It was so bad that when my parents brought my brother to the hospital, the doctor there said Samrakhan would never walk again. They refused to believe this news and brought him to see the shaman, who said, just as they entered his home, "I have been waiting for you."

The shaman prayed over some mare's milk, which is already considered holy in our culture. That is the milk of the female horse. We drink it on special occasions. This shaman used it as his medicine and told my mother to give it to Samrakhan first thing in the morning and last thing at night. His neck healed quickly after that.

My mother said the shaman had the spirit. He came from three generations of shamans and was powerful.

The shaman rubbed my mother's pregnant belly with yak butter and performed a ritual around her that included chanting and the burning of a special herb. Then he wrapped her belly with fabric, "to hold the baby up high in her womb," he said.

He also ordered my mom to rest. For a nomad woman, this is very difficult. But she took him seriously, as did my father, and his parents, and her parents, who started visiting regularly to help my father with all the chores that my mother usually did. These included cooking and cleaning and milking the cows and turning that milk into soft and hard cheeses. It also meant collecting the dung patties that were being air-dried in the special corral outside our house to make the coal to heat our home. My mother was also responsible for sewing clothes for my brother and father, and for herself, and making the felt from lamb's wool and the blankets from

THE WHITE EAGLE

sheepskin and other animal hides that we use to keep warm at night. We also use them as insulation to keep our spring and autumn homes warm. The list of things Kazakh women do is very long.

The bigger she got with me, the more the shaman encouraged my mother to keep still.

She worried that she would lose me as she had the others.

So when my grandmother arrived, after my mother had carried me for nine months, and reported that she had seen the White Eagle in her dreams, my mother felt relief for the first time during that entire pregnancy.

"This baby will bring luck to our household," my grandmother announced that same day.

The very next morning, on May 9, 2001, I was born.

Or, as my mother says, "I was ready to see the light."

This is the expression we use when a baby comes into the world.

My mom was ready, too. But our car was not. My father could not get it to start! Instead, he had to ride his horse to the hospital, an hour away, and fetch someone on a motorbike to come back with him, and then ride my mother on this same motorbike back to the hospital in Altansogts, the nearest town.

When they arrived, my father barely got her up the stairs to the gurney awaiting her. I was born before they even entered the birthing room.

News of my birth traveled quickly, and family members came to the hospital to meet me. My mother's brother was the one who came up with my name.

Aisholpan means "Venus moon," the one star you see in the sky all the time, no matter what time of year. It is how nomads tell time. It guides us.

My uncle said, "Aisholpan will guide us. She will be shiny, like this star."

The curse had been broken.

My mother could return home to her nomadic

way of life and continue to build her family. As for me, my mother says that, despite my harrowing arrival, I was an easy child.

"You rarely cried," my mom said. "We could leave you inside at home all day to go get the sheep from the mountains. And when we would come home, you would still be in the same spot. Staring out the window. Never moving. Just waiting for us to come back."

My father insists that my calm nature is why I was such a natural with eagles.

2

My People Are Eagle Hunters

For a time, long before I was born, eagle hunting was banned in Mongolia. From 1924, after World War I, until 1989, after the collapse of the Soviet Union, the Communists in power decreed it illegal, punishable by time in prison. The way my father explained it to me was that the Communists believed that everyone should live the same life—which meant that any cultural practice, such as eagle hunting for my people or the Buddhist religion for the Mongol people who were the majority in Mongolia, was outlawed. It also meant that nomads no longer owned their herds—the government did. This was a very difficult period for the Kazakh people.

Kazakhs lived for centuries with no homeland, roaming the land between the Altai Mountains and the Black Sea. This is why Kazakh nomads now live in China, Mongolia, and Kazakhstan. We were never people to be contained by borders. It wasn't until the early 1900s that Mongolia offered citizenship to the Kazakh nomads in the northwestern region of the country.

But in 1924, the new Communist ruler led a brutal purge of Kazakhs, as well as Buddhists. Nomads raised livestock for self-reliance, but the new laws mandated that their livestock was now property of the Communist regime. Livestock exports to Russia rose dramatically—and, understandably, the Kazakh nomads revolted. Instead of living off the land, every single citizen had to register with the government and perform an assigned government job. People who disobeyed wound up in prison or dead. They were dark times.

Life under communism was all my mom and dad had known.

My father's father worked for the government as a commissioner for the district. As part of his job, he had to shoot marmots, foxes, and wolves for their pelts—not for his family, but for the government. He often brought my father along because my father was a good shooter. So as a teenager, my father hunted with guns for the government. And since the Altai Mountains are so remote, and therefore the risk of being caught was slim, my grandfather would also bring his eagle.

My grandfather is one of the reasons eagle hunting is still practiced in Mongolia today.

He and others like him continued the tradition in secret. He taught my father, as well as his other sons, how to hunt with eagles just as his father had

MY PEOPLE ARE EAGLE HUNTERS

taught him—despite the fact that if he or any of his sons got caught, they would have gone to jail.

My grandfather risked it because, as he always said, eagle hunting was in our family's blood. He kept his eagle in hiding. The end of communism meant no longer having to hide his eagle or this tradition. This was great for my father and his siblings. They no longer had to hunt in secret.

My father can name eagle hunters in our family for all seven generations that precede him, all of them men. I am part of the eighth generation.

All my childhood memories involve an eagle. I have never, ever been scared of eagles. I have been up close to them since before I can remember.

"When you first started to crawl, you went right to my eagle," my father often says.

This still makes him so proud: His eagle was my playmate. During the winter months, she lived inside our home with us, on her perch, and, according to my parents, I always wanted to play near her. When I started talking, I talked to her, and she would chirp at me, bobbing back and forth, side to side. I was so in love with his bird that my father let me help feed her before I turned one. I held the meat in one hand as my father held my wrist, and I watched, delighted, as the bird pecked at her food.

My dad's bird was as tall as I was at one year old. Her wingspan was six feet wide, the same length as my father was standing up; her beak was so sharp, it could slice through skin down to the bone; and her talons were so strong, they could snap a finger or an arm. As proof, my father has scars up and down his arms, and is missing the bottom chunk of his earlobe.

"I was helping my friend train his eagle," he explains whenever anyone asks about his deformed ear, "and his eagle got angry with me."

We both find this so funny. Eagles have personalities, and this one was particularly feisty! My dad did not blame the eagle. He always says that it is the

MY PEOPLE ARE EAGLE HUNTERS

responsibility of the trainer or hunter to treat his bird with respect, no matter what.

My dad has had eight eagles over his lifetime—and he claims that each had a distinct way of being. They are like any creature. Some are lazy. Others are fierce. Some are sweet.

It depends on their nature and how you treat them.

My dad's earliest memories are like mine—there was always an eagle in the house during the winter, and outside during the warmer summer months. My mother, however, did not have any eagle hunters in her family, so living with an eagle was entirely new to her. In fact, she had never even seen an eagle up close until she married my dad.

Summer is the one time of the year when eagle hunters *don't* hunt—and that was the season when my parents married. My father had an eagle at the time who was living outside at his parents' home—where he and my mother first lived together—either on her perch or in her own small ger, to keep her protected from the wind at night. That fall, my parents moved to a plot of land at the base of the small hill, where my father began building their winter home. The eagle came with them. This is our home today.

It started as a small room, which my father built from wood and stucco mud. Since there was no extra ger for his eagle, the bird lived in the house—with them.

My mother was newly wed, with a one-room house that was big enough to fit the stove, their marriage bed, and a separate cot for visiting relatives—and the tughir, or perch, which was passed down to my father from his father. My father placed it in the corner near their bed. And then my mother moved it to the far corner, as far away from the bed as possible.

"I was so scared of what the bird might do to me," she said. "It was big! And had the sharpest beak. And she would look at me in a way that intimidated me. After all, I was the newcomer!"

My mother said that she soon grew accustomed to living with the bird.

"She was a very calm bird," she says. "She chirped from time to time, but that was it. And your father loved the bird so much. Every night, he would sit and talk to her, stroking her head. She would bob back and forth, chirping to him. I went from being a little jealous to falling in love with the bird, and with your father's love for her."

By the time my brother was born, in 1992, my mother knew in her heart that the eagle would never hurt him or her.

If you ask her about any of our eagles today, she says, "The eagle is part of the family. They're holy birds."

I was four years old when my brother trapped his first eagle. Samrakhan was thirteen, the age when boys are traditionally taught by their fathers about eagle hunting. I remember him bringing her home and the look of pride on his face. I was small but knew even then that I would catch my own eagle one day. That was my dream.

I looked up to my big brother. He was quiet and calm, always. A lot like me. He also encouraged me to watch him learn. Both he and my father thought it was funny that I, a pudgy small girl, loved eagles as much as I did. Samrakhan let me play with his eaglet, just as my father let me play with his older eagle.

I did not know then that this was a tradition passed down from father to son. I was too young to understand that. But I did think, as most four-year-olds do, that I could do anything a boy could do.

After all, I come from a long line of eagle hunters. We do not back down from a challenge.

3

Nomadic Life

Despite occasional hunger, my memories from childhood are otherwise happy.

I especially enjoyed helping my parents with all our animals. Before I was even one year old, my father would bring me on his horse to herd the goats. I got my own pony soon after that—every nomad child has a pony. That is how we get around. It is our way of life. I started riding my pony when I was four and could gallop by the time I was six. I became a jockey when I was eight years old and, according to my dad, was very good. I entered horse-racing contests and won often.

We do not name our horses. Instead, we call them by their colors. Brown. Black. White with spots. Some of our favorite horses will be named, but even then, it is always something descriptive, such as Black Stallion. Or Trottero for a horse who always trots, never gallops. When I think back to being a little kid, I think of galloping across the steppes on my pony. This, to me, is freedom.

In a funny twist, my sister is named Saigulikh, which means "fast colt."

When my mother was pregnant with Saigulikh, my father had a beautiful and very fast horse. My mother was nine months pregnant and felt ready to give birth. But there was a very important horse race that was taking place in Ölgii. The prizes were cash, and my father knew he could win with his horse. So he asked my mother to wait one day before giving birth so he could go and compete.

It takes six hours to get to Ölgii by horse, so he went that night, raced the following morning, and won! When he returned home later that evening, no one was there.

"Your mother did not listen to me," he says whenever he tells this story. "She could not wait."

"Saigulikh could not wait!" my mother teases back.

Hence her name.

My brother Dinka was born three years after Saigulikh. This, my parents say, proves that I was the beginning of their good luck.

But there are hard memories, too.

I remember being hungry.

And I remember the harsh winters that stole our animals from us.

My parents tell stories from the years before I was born that were dire. They call the period from 1993 to 2000 the starvation times. Frigid storms arrived right after communism ended, which was doubly difficult as nomads went back to their herding and grazing, whereas under a communist government everyone had an assigned job, through the state.

A combination of circumstances, beginning with drought in the summer, meant that the grass was not as abundant, and as a result, our animals went into the winter thinner than usual. And then *dzud* hit. Dzud is a winter storm that plunges the temperatures to negative sixty degrees Fahrenheit. If the goats and sheep and cows are too thin, they have no fat to keep them warm. They freeze to death.

We depend on our animals, so if they suffer, we suffer, too.

People had less to eat because of dzud. Nomads back then depended on their animals to eat and to trade for basics, such as flour and salt and tea. It got a bit better after I was born—but by this point, so many nomads had given up their way of life. All my mother's siblings had moved to Kazakhstan, a nation that formed after the Soviet Union collapsed. An invitation from the new government went out to any Kazakh people, saying they were welcome. Many nomads accepted the offer, trading their gers and ponies for apartments and motorbikes. Some nomads chose to stay in Mongolia, but moved instead to apartments or homes in Ölgii or even as far away as Ulanbataar, the capital of Mongolia, where they often wound up living in tent slums on the outskirts of the capital without any of their animals or means to make a living.

This never even crossed my father's or my mother's minds. My mother married my father because she loved the nomad life. And my father would say this is the only life he ever wanted to live.

For my family, it is almost impossible to imagine a life without animals.

This is how we have lived for centuries. This is all we know.

THE EAGLE HUNTRESS

I used to play a lot in the mountains with Saigulikh and Dinka. We each always had our own pony and would ride for hours. Before we left home, we would stuff our pockets with the hard, sour-tasting rock cheese that my mom made from the curds of goat's or cow's milk. They looked like stones and were so hard, you could chip a tooth on them if you were not careful. That taste to me is happiness. It reminds me of my childhood, before the tourists came. Before a movie was made of my life. Before I was famous.

Back when it was just me living a nomad girl's life. I had never heard of New York City or Los Angeles, let alone imagined ever visiting either place. My siblings and I had never heard of a hamburger or pizza, or even seen candy! Or gum!

Everything we ate, we made ourselves.

When I was eight and Saigulikh was five, we

started going to Altansogts Secondary School, which was in the nearest village. Before that, I went to school in Ölgii, the nearest big town for one hundred miles. I would board during the week and come home on the weekends. But I was lonely. I missed my family. So when Saigulikh turned five and was ready to start school, my parents decided to switch us to both go to the local boarding school. Altansogts was only four miles from our winter house, as opposed to Ölgii, which is roughly forty miles away. Most of the students at Altansogts were from nomadic families and, like us, they spent the weekdays in the two-story dormitory.

My father would ride me and Saigulikh on his motorbike to drop us off on Sunday night and pick us up on Friday afternoon. It was a short ride—only fifteen minutes—compared with the hour walk, and my sister and I loved it. My father sat my sister in front of him on the padded seat, and I climbed on the back, behind him, and held on to his waist as we bumped our way over the tire-track-grooved, dirt-packed road. The hum of the motorcycle coupled with the sand-colored dust clouds kicked up by its wheels was a soundtrack to the happiness I felt heading to school to see all my friends. When we moved to our autumn ger at the end of summer, we could walk to school, and we grazed our animals in a valley that was less than a mile away. That walk was also so lovely, over the rolling green pastures dotted with cows, listening to the clinking of bells some of them wore around their necks to help herders know where they had wandered to.

School started every morning at six thirty. Our alarm clock was a teacher pounding on the door.

Thud, thud, thud!

My eyes would shoot open at the first knock, and I would fling off my sheets as quickly as possible—the faster I got out of bed, the sooner I got to use the washroom. There was only one per floor, for more than two dozen girls.

I'd brush my teeth and wash my face before

getting dressed for school. We did not wear uniforms at this school, so I would put on my pants, shirt, and a sweater before going to the dining room for breakfast. There, I sat with Saigulikh and our friends, who were all from nomadic families like ours. We would eat bread with butter and drink tea, then go to our first class at eight thirty. We took math, Mongolian, science, and history classes through one PM and then took a break for lunch. The afternoon was dedicated to sports.

I did fine in class but really excelled in sports. Volleyball was my favorite. I also liked judo because I was so good at it. My grandfather taught me how to wrestle when I was very young, and he was so proud of me because I often beat my older male cousins in the family tournaments that he oversaw when all of us were together at the spring and summer pastures. The same was true at school. Most kids, boys or girls, were scared to wrestle me because they knew I would win.

We would break for dinner at five and then settle into our dorm rooms—girls in one building, boys in another—doing our homework, braiding one another's hair, or playing chess or backgammon. I loved those cozy nights gossiping with friends.

I liked being at school but could not wait to go home on the weekends. My happy place was on my pony, riding in the steppes or helping my father take care of his eagle.

He let me feed her and sometimes he even let me practice calling to her by dragging a rabbit skin behind me as I jogged away from her, summoning her to fly from her perch to the pelt. This was one of the ways my father worked with the bird to keep her in good shape for hunting.

I was always thrilled when he let me help him.

"You are good with my bird," my dad would say. "You have a gift."

I don't know what that gift was other than a deep love for eagles, so much so that when Samrakhan was called away to do his army service (every male in Mongolia has to do a year in the army when he turns eighteen), he asked me to take care of *his* bird, too.

The week before my brother left, he asked if I could do this for him. I had just turned ten.

"Feed her every few days," he said. "Not too much, she needs time to digest."

He was telling me how to do all these things that I had already learned from my father, but I let him. I was just so happy that I would get to take care of her all by myself. My mind was racing about all the things I might do with her, when he snapped me back to attention.

"She really likes it when you rub her neck," he said, demonstrating as he explained. "Not too rough; gently but firmly rub on the top of her head down her neck."

I tried it myself and I felt her strong but small skull pushing into my hand beneath her downy layer of gray and brown feathers.

"That's right," my brother said, smiling. Pleased.

"I will take great care of you!" I said as she bowed her head for another rub. "I promise."

Eagles eat meat, so my father would cut a chunk of rabbit or goat into small pieces, which I would then skewer on the end of a long, pointy stick. We also have a special bowl carved out of wood called a *saptiayahk*, which makes it easy to give them water. I would feed Samrakhan's eagle on Friday as soon as I got home and not again until I left late Sunday. My father would feed her in the middle of the week.

I also helped my dad herd the goats and sheep, which meant spending many afternoons on my horse, riding with my dad over the ridges in search of the herds. I learned so much from my father about how to read the landscape: to follow stars that pointed in specific directions, even when faded in the daylight sky; and how turning left at the knotted tree trunk would take you to the river, which zigzags to the best watering hole, where we would likely find the cows.

NOMADIC LIFE

"The world is our map," my father liked to say.

My other chores included milking the cows, then helping my mom turn the milk into butter and cheeses, including the rock cheese I loved. My least favorite job was shoveling the cow and horse dung patties we used as fuel for our stoves.

I liked helping my mother with laundry—hand-washing our clothes in a big corrugated tub of water with soap and then laying the clothes to dry over the stone wall behind our house. In the winter months, the sweaters and jeans would freeze into human shapes and I would have to bring them back indoors to thaw and warm up before they could be folded and put away.

Once the school year ended, we all went home to help pack up to make the move to Olun Noor, our spring pasture. I love it there, as that is where we and our relatives meet up, five families in all. This is a happy time for my family.

My parents have a large wooden trunk, which they fill with our ger—the wooden frame, felt, animal pelts, and canvas that complete it—as well as the beds, rugs, dishes, kitchen utensils, and stove to transport to the spring and summer pastures.

Before my dad had his four-wheel-drive truck, he would load the trunk with all our belongings onto one of our camels.

At one point in my life, we had three camels, and I still miss them. They are such stubborn, funny, strong creatures. And so fast! One of my favorite games is camel racing. I am really good at it: You sit in front of the hump, at the base of the camel's neck, legs straddling each side. The key is to stay calm, always. Camels are sensitive, like horses. They are also stubborn. If they don't want to move, they won't budge.

When we made the move to the spring pasture, the trunks were placed on top of the camels, and then Saigulikh, Dinka, and I would climb on top of it. We would ride that way for the two days it took to get to Olon Nuur, where we would meet my grandparents, aunts, uncles, and cousins. All our gers would be set up near one another, which meant family dinners and games every day. Like the camel races. And wrestling matches.

My grandfather's winter home was ten miles away from ours, so we did not get to see him too often. This was due not so much to the distance as to how hard we all worked to keep our animals well fed and safe during those bitter cold months.

We stayed in Olon Nuur for ten to twenty days to let our animals eat before making the three-day trek into the Altai Mountains, to a beautiful place called Tekht, our summer pasture.

Our eagles come with us every time we move, but in the summer, we don't hunt with them. Eagle hunting is done only in the wintertime, when foxes are easiest to spot against the pure white snow and their fur is thick for protection from the cold temperatures. So, as we do with our other animals, we let our eagles fatten up, too.

These summer months are good for our spirits, and for our animals as well. It is a time to be with family, and the animals can feast on the sweet summer grass and get fat in preparation for the tough winter months ahead.

4

A Rite of Passage

I spent a lot of time watching my brother train his eagle. He got his first eagle when he was thirteen. I was five. I watched him and my father out in the front of our winter house, one of them dragging a fox pelt while the other released the eagle to get her used to flying short distances.

When I was eight, my father finally let me ride up into the mountains with him and Samrakhan. I wanted to see how each called to their eagles out in the wild.

I was still too young to be the scarer—the person who rides ahead on horseback and tries to scare the fox out if its den—but I loved seeing my dad gallop down a hill where he thought a fox might be, and I loved hearing his voice fill the air. I studied the look on my brother's face as he launched his eagle into the air: It was pure joy. I could not wait to do it myself one day.

Back then, it never even occurred to me that I wouldn't. That some in our community would object to my becoming an eagle hunter just because I am a girl.

By the time my brother went into the army, he was a full-fledged eagle hunter. My father had seen him through all the stages, beginning with caring for his eagle, then becoming a scarer, and finally taking him on his first winter hunt. That was when

A RITE OF PASSAGE

my father led him up to the Altai Mountains to catch a fox in the snow. That is what makes you a real eagle hunter.

Samrakhan was sad to leave his eagle behind when he left for the army. He was otherwise excited to go—he could have postponed one year, to start at nineteen, but he wanted to do his service. I witnessed not only the training but also the relationship that grew between him and his bird. Love and respect. Those are the words that come to mind.

From the time Samrakhan brought home the eaglet that he'd caught, I knew I wanted to follow in his and our father's footsteps. I was happy to take care of his eagle while he was gone, but I also wondered, *When will I be able to get my own eagle?*

I finally asked my father, "How can I be a real eagle huntress?"

After spending another day watching my father and his friends fly their eagles in the wild, I summoned the courage to ask this. I knew I could do it if given the chance. And I was the right age, as most boys start training at twelve or thirteen. I was twelve. I was ready.

By then, I knew that eagle hunting was something that was passed down from father to son. Daughters were not part of the tradition. But I also knew that both my father and grandfather admired how strong I was and how calm I was around eagles. My gifts, they both told me.

My father considered my request. I thought I noticed a sparkle in his eye. But he remained silent.

I was patient with eagles but not with fathers. "Will you teach me?" I asked. "Or are you against me?"

My father remained silent. I turned away from him.

"Aisholpan!" he finally said. "You are strong!"

I smiled, just a small one.

"You carry my eagle and your brother's eagle well," he continued. "You are not afraid, which is the biggest thing."

A RITE OF PASSAGE

My heart started to beat a bit faster.

"But there has never been a female hunter in our family," he said.

The conversation was taking a hard turn.

Just then, my mother walked in carrying a bowl with a goat leg sticking out of it.

"Still, I will consider teaching you," he said.

"Teach her what?" my mother asked as she placed the bowl on the kitchen table.

"Aisholpan wants to learn how to hunt with eagles," my father responded.

My mother took in what my father said, tucked her chin to her chest, and kept quiet for a moment. I could tell from her silence that something about my request was bothering her.

"It's one thing to feed and work with the eagle here at home," she finally said, keeping her head down. "Or to go and watch your father and his friends hunt. But taking your own bird into the mountains to hunt is tiring—and dangerous."

My father was about to say yes to a dream I had

had since I could remember having dreams. The idea that my mother would get in the way made me feel panicky.

"Aisholpan is very strong," my father countered. I was glad he spoke before I did. I had all these thoughts rushing to take shape into words.

"She is the best horse rider in the family," he added. "Almost as good as me."

He shot me a look and winked.

That eased the tension in my throat and helped untangle the words caught in my mouth.

"I can ride my pony for hours, herding," I said to my mom. "And have carried baby goats, which weigh more than an eagle, for miles. You know I am strong enough."

My mother sighed. "This is not something I imagined for you, Aisholpan," she said. "I worry enough when your father and brother go out on long hunts. Now I must worry about you as well?"

"Is it because I am a girl?" I asked.

I was confused and angered by my mother's

hesitation. She had always supported me, even during the wrestling matches against my cousins. I did not understand why she was not supporting me now.

"Aisholpan," my father interjected, "your mother has reason to worry. This is not an easy thing you are asking us to consider."

Now I was losing my father, too. This was not going as I had hoped.

"To be a true eagle huntress, you must do more than call your eagle to a pelt," my father said.

"I know!" I must have shouted, because both my parents looked at me with surprise in their faces.

I'd never shouted at them. They looked at each other, and something I couldn't decipher passed between them.

"You must be able to ride with your eagle in the wintertime," my father continued, "when the snow is deep and the air so cold it freezes your horse's breath into icicles. That is the true test of a hunter, and his eagle."

"What about *her* eagle?" I countered, feeling the anger rise in me. I accepted, finally, that the only reason they were hesitating was because I was a girl.

"The winters are brutally cold," my mother added. "And in the mountains, with no shelter from the wind or snow... I get worried that it will be too much for you."

Our winters are cold, it is true. The snow can sometimes be taller than your horse. But that did not scare me. Why did it scare her? My whole body tensed up as she spoke. I was not expecting her to be against me.

My mother had started making dinner. It was *besbarmak*, which means "five-finger meal" in Kazakh, a meat-and-noodle stew we eat with our hands. It is a very special dish, one she usually made when we were expecting visitors.

"I can do it," I said. "Please let me try. Father said he would train—"

"I said I would consider it," he said. "But your mother must say it's okay."

A RITE OF PASSAGE

As we were talking, she bent over the kitchen table, forming the dough that she made from flour and water into a big ball in her hands and then flattening it out by rolling a smooth piece of wood over it before it would be cut into noodles for the stew. This is one of my favorite dishes. She went to place the goat leg in the pot that was simmering away on the stove. Our home quickly filled with the scent of meat broth, ready for the noodles to be boiled alongside the bits of goat that fell from the bone as it cooked. My stomach growled in response, hungry for dinner.

My father listened to my mother and me quarrel, shook his head, and then headed out, leaving us in our standoff.

I sat on the edge of my parents' bed, simmering like the besbarmak. What if my father agreed with my mother? How could I convince her that I was strong enough to do it? How would I ever forgive her? I was getting so upset, my whole body began to tremble.

"I can see that you are disappointed." My mother's gentle voice penetrated the thoughts swarming through my head like hornets. "And I know you have a special talent," she continued, and my ears perked up as I noticed a shift in her tone.

I turned to face her.

"You say that your father is not against you?" she asked, slicing the now-thin, disk-shaped dough into long strands for the stew, not once looking up at me as she spoke.

"He wants to teach me," I said. "Ask him yourself."

At that moment, we heard the door squeak open and thump shut, followed by the stamping of my father's big boots and the high-pitched chirps of his eagle. He emerged through the interior door with his eagle bobbing her head back and forth.

"Has your mother softened?" he asked me with a smile.

His eagle stopped chirping.

A RITE OF PASSAGE

"You must ask her!" I replied, and looked at him with my eyes stretched wide. I needed his support.

"Alma!" he said as he sat down at the table. My mother was now placing the noodles in the boiling pot. Dinner would be ready soon. "Aisholpan really wants to learn to become an eagle huntress."

"She has made that very clear," my mother responded, now pouring tea into his bowl.

"Ever since she was a baby, I have been watching her talent with eagles," he said before taking his first slurp. "She is a natural."

My mother went quiet again. I stood up to get my own bowl to have tea. I was suddenly thirsty.

"If you really believe she can do this," my mother said, finally, "then I will not be against it."

The relief I felt in that moment was so great, I almost dropped my tea bowl.

"Rakmet!" I may have shouted a million thank-yous as I placed the bowl on the table with shaky hands and got up to hug my mother to show my appreciation. When I looked up at her, my eyes were glassy with tears. I saw that hers were, too.

"You must promise to be extra careful, Aisholpan," she said as she hugged me back.

I was smiling so hard by then, thinking about what this meant, that my cheeks pushed my moist eyes closed, forcing a tear to run down my face. My mother wiped it away as I said, "I promise!"

My dad was smiling, too. He took another sip of tea and nodded at me.

"We can start tomorrow," he said with a wink.

5

Tourists

Visitors had started coming when I was very young, but they were coming more frequently now—especially over the summer and fall months. These were not family members or neighbors. These were tourists.

My mother cooked for them, and my father took them out on a hunt. My brother used to do this with him. Now it was my turn. My father said I could be the scarer on the next tourist expedition.

That night, waiting for the tourists to come, I could barely contain my excitement.

The first time I saw a tourist, I was five years old. He had arrived from Ölgii on horseback with a Mongolian translator who spoke Kazakh and a very funny-sounding language that I now know is English. Kazakhs are a minority in Mongolia, where the national language is Mongolian. We learn it in school, and every Kazakh is expected to know how to speak it, but the reverse is not true. Not many Mongolians speak Kazakh, so this was already strange, to have a Mongolian man we had never seen before speaking Kazakh in our home. But even more strange was that he was speaking a completely foreign language to a man who looked as funny as he sounded. He was tall and so pale, like a ghost with a mop of golden autumn grass–colored hair. He was also dressed in such odd clothes, made from a shiny, puffy material I had never seen before.

TOURISTS

He kept smiling and nodding at us, and speaking this funny language to the Mongolian man, who kept laughing and speaking back to him in gibberish. Then this glow-in-the-dark ghost man took a small black box out of his bag, put it up to his face, and pointed it at me. I heard a clicking sound, and then a bright light filled the room, like a flash of lightning that sent a shock throughout my whole body.

I was so scared that I burst into tears.

My father laughed—so did the tourist and the translator. But my mother was also upset. She put her arm around me and shouted at my father to stop laughing, while staring sternly at this stranger with his flashing machine. I kept crying.

My dad tells this story all the time. He thinks it is so funny, and I do, too, now that I have met hundreds, if not thousands, of tourists who have visited my home and taken my photo.

At first I did not understand why everyone was so interested in seeing how Kazakh nomads live:

Yes, we live in one room, and sleep on mats, and eat the animals we raise. Yes, we live with eagles, and hunt with them, too. And, yes, we use the fur from the fox and rabbit and wolf that our eagles catch to make our coats and hats. This is and has always been my life, so it was fascinating to me that it was so fascinating to them—to the point that they paid real money to live with us for a few days for the "nomad experience."

We have gotten used to it by now.

It is not unusual to have four or more strangers sleeping in our one-room home, side by side in their sleeping bags. These people—mostly from North America, but also from Europe and other parts of Asia—have been coming for years now. They bring rice or cooking oil or money in exchange for spending a night or several. They want to eat our food and drink our salt tea or fermented mare's milk, a delicacy. They want to live the way we live.

During the hunger years, these visits were a lifeline. The money that tourists paid to stay with nomad families helped these families, mine included, to survive.

My father often tells the story of the first time he saw a tourist. The man's name was Zeep, and he came on horseback with a translator.

That first night, for dinner, my mother made a stew out of cow intestines—we eat every part of the animal, not just the meat. When my father invited Zeep to stay and eat, he said he was not hungry, which my parents found strange.

"He had been riding for hours in quite cold conditions," my father remembers.

"How is he not hungry?" my mother asked the translator.

"He is not used to the food we eat," the translator explained.

Zeep stayed the night, and when my parents were ready to go to sleep, he rolled out a funny-looking bag that was long and thin. He placed it on the floor, next to my parents' bed because the house was so small—there was nowhere else to go—then zipped himself in and closed his eyes.

Not much time had passed when my dad woke up to find Zeep shivering because he was so cold. My dad laid an animal hide on him—this is how we keep warm—and the next thing he knew, Zeep was snoring so loudly that he woke up my mother, who thought an animal was in the house. They still laugh about this.

Zeep is a very important person—or VIP, as my dad says—as his visit was the beginning of our good relationship with tourists. He came for one night and wound up staying for twenty days.

My dad had a Russian motorbike at the time and drove Zeep around the steppes and showed him how we herd and care for our animals. Zeep was amazed at how beautiful Bayan-Ölgii was. He said it looked like the moon, which my father also thought was funny.

TOURISTS

"Have you been to the moon?" my dad asked him. "How do you know what it looks like?"

Teasing aside, my dad said it was fun to have this foreign visitor.

"He was so amazed by things that are no big deal to us," my dad recalls. "That the stars in the sky are our maps. That we put salt in our tea. That we hunt with eagles and wear the pelts we catch. What is fascinating to them is normal to us. It is our life!"

The next time Zeep came back, the following year, it was with three other people who looked a lot like him and who also were interested in the nomad experience. They stayed for ten days, and this time, my dad showed them how he hunted with his eagle.

"People could not believe their eyes," my father recalls. "From that moment on, it became the thing everyone wanted to see."

It was the very thing I would get to do with my father now.

We saddled up six ponies in preparation for the tourists we knew would be coming. I would get to be the scarer, just as my dad had promised.

Several hours later, we saw the dust rising in the distance. A gray van barreled toward us. As it approached, my father and I laid out our outfits for the hunt. My mother put on the kettle for tea.

The van pulled up in front of the house and three tourists piled out of the backseat.

Their translator was someone we knew well. He introduced us to this new group: two men in their thirties and a woman in her forties, all visiting from Canada. We greeted them and invited them into the house to eat bread with yak butter and drink salt tea. Then we went back outside to mount the waiting ponies.

My father called to me, "Aisholpan, bring me my eagle!"

I went to her perch, where she was waiting with her hood still on.

We call the mask eagles wear a *tomaga*, which is made of cowhide. It keeps the eagle calm. I then coaxed her onto my right arm by placing it near her feet. I was wearing my brother's *biyalai*, the glove made of goatskin to protect against the eagle's sharp claws. The glove covered my brother's forearm, but since my arm was smaller, it went past my elbow. As the eagle stepped onto the glove, I picked up each of her feet with my free hand to wrap each taloned toe securely around my forearm.

In the meantime, my father had mounted his pony and was attaching the *baldahk*, or leaning stick, to the saddle. It is made of river birch and has a padded cushion that rests on the horse's shoulder. This is where an eagle hunter can rest the hand he uses to hold the eagle when he goes on long treks. I passed the eagle to my father, who had his biyalai on, and then went to mount my pony.

I saw that the tourists' faces had lit up and heard them chatting to one another in an animated way, but I had no idea what they were saying. All I knew was that they seemed as excited as I felt—I was finally getting to do something I had dreamed about since I was small. Seeing these strangers' feelings matching my own made me realize that this was a big deal, after all. I was going to participate on an eagle hunt.

All these thoughts ran through my mind as I followed my father on his horse up into the surrounding hills, with the three tourists and the translator in tow.

We rode for about forty-five minutes before we arrived at the top of a hill where my dad thought there might be a fox. They like to burrow and make dens in the crevices between the shale rock. My dad gave me the signal—*"Hup!"*—which meant I should start galloping in a zigzag down the hill.

The point is to scare the foxes out of their dens. I had seen my brother do this countless times and

TOURISTS

thought I could do it. Now was my chance. I dug my heels into my pony to get her started. *"Hiya!"*

I galloped and shouted, scanning the area for any movement. I knew that this could take many attempts. The goal is to scare the fox (or rabbit or wolf cub or wolf, for that matter) out of its burrow.

Once I see any movement, my job is to signal to my father, who would then take the hood off his eagle and release her into the air to hunt.

We had no luck on that first hill, so we went to another ridge nearby and did the same routine. This time, I saw a flash of fur in the distance. I signaled to my father, who quickly set his eagle on course with a strong "Huka!" cry, the sound eagle hunters make to activate their eagles.

The hunt was on!

Watching the eagle take flight from my father's arm is still one of my favorite things. She spread her wings, then launched straight up, like a rocket, into the sky, where she scanned the horizon, looking for that same flash of orangey-brown, silver fox.

I saw her spot it, then circle again, looking for the best attack route before plummeting beak first through the air, as if she were diving toward the ground.

Her eagle eyes were focused on the fox, her beak pointed toward it like a bow trained on a target. As she closed in on her prey, she flipped her body so suddenly that her feet faced the fox, which had stood up on its hind legs in self-defense. That gave the eagle a clean target—she grabbed its neck with one claw, its chest with the other, and quickly killed it by puncturing its heart and lungs with her talons.

My heart seemed to be racing as fast as my pony could gallop as we rode toward the eagle, now bowing over the dead fox. I saw my father galloping there as well. The thrill on his face matched mine.

I watched in awe as his eagle remained stationary, her talons gripping the now-limp fox. Never once did she he even try to peck at its flesh. She seemed to know intuitively to keep the pelt intact, as that is the prize—a pristine fur to turn into a hat or coat. This is the most amazing trait about the eagle, my father says. She is that smart.

My father arrived and jumped off his horse, grabbing a rabbit leg out of the bag he wore strapped to his chest. This pouch is called a *djem khlata*, or "food sack," which is made specifically for transporting food for the eagle. Since hunters hunt in the winter, when it is freezing cold, the bag is lined with felt to prevent the meat from freezing.

My father knelt on one knee, with the rabbit leg in the gloved hand, and waved it below his eagle's beak. That seemed to snap her out of her reverie. She perked up and started tearing at the rabbit leg with her beak.

That was when my father bowed his head and cupped his hands to pray. "It is the law of nature."

We say this to praise both creatures, the fox and the eagle. It's similar to our tradition before we slaughter an animal for food, when we say, "Forgive us. You are a pure creature. It is not because you have sinned; it is because we are hungry."

By then, the Canadian tourists had arrived on their ponies and were snapping photos and marveling at what just had happened.

As we rode home, my father and I were discussing what I had just seen.

"She knew exactly what to do," I said, still marveling at the eagle's speed in killing the fox.

"This is her natural ability," he replied. "As a hunter, you just want to create the space for your eagle to be able to do what she does in the wild."

The tourists had so many more questions than I did—I had grown up knowing about eagle hunting, but for them, this was brand-new. A miracle witnessed.

We'd had so many tourists visit us by then that my dad was used to their questions and curiosity. The people who came to stay with us were often as kind as they were curious.

One year, there was a doctor in the group. By that time, my father's mother was going blind. She was having a very hard time getting around and could no longer sew, which is what she was known for. Her beautiful Kazakh quilts decorate our ger. The doctor who was visiting noticed this and asked if he could look at her eyes. The translator explained that he might have a way to help my grandmother see again.

After he examined her eyes, he said to my father, "I can help her."

He arranged for my grandmother to go to Ulaanbaatar. That meant driving for seven hours to a town called Khovd, where my grandmother still had to take an airplane for another four hours to get to the capital city. The doctor promised that the trip would be worth it.

In Kazakh, there was no word for cataracts. We say, she has the white dots in her eyes.

My grandmother agreed to go.

Once she arrived, they did an operation and she could see. It was like magic.

"She could sew again!" my father says so proudly. "She made coats and hats with fox and wolf fur and did Kazakh embroidery until the day she died."

This tourist gave my grandmother more than her sight back.

He also began visiting often. When he learned that my grandmother had died, he came to pay his respects.

"He was crying," my father remembers.

He still comes to visit and brings doctors with him to help both Mongolian and Kazakh people.

My father says that working with these foreign people was a blessing. We learned about new cultures through them, and they learned about Kazakh culture through us. They also brought so many things, whether flour, or tea, or honey—as well as candies, pens, and paper. Toothbrushes and toothpaste. Things we had never seen or used before.

TOURISTS

I have so many happy memories of all the different people who have stayed with us.

I have met people from Canada and the United States as well as many from Europe, South America, and Asia. I learned more about these different cultures, and about basic geography, than I did at school.

Most of the people who visited were my parents' age—so much older than me. But there was one girl who visited when I was about ten years old who was exactly my age. She said she was from Australia, and I thought that was her name!

I introduced her to Saigulikh as "Australia," and the two of us called her that all morning until the translator overheard us and said, "No, she is *from* Australia!"

Saigulikh asked, "What is Australia?"

The translator explained that it was a country that was ten hours away by airplane—and that was just to get to Ulaanbaatar! It took another four hours to get from UB to Ölgii! And an hour to drive to visit us.

"She must really have wanted to meet us!" Saigulikh joked.

"What is her name?" I asked the translator.

"Yuki!" he said.

Yuki and her family stayed with us for several days, and I still remember how much fun we had. Even though we could not speak to one another, we were able to use body language to communicate. I felt that she understood me.

Saigulikh and I took her horseback riding and let her help us herd the baby goats in the pasture. She also helped us collect the dung patties and place them in the corral to dry out. I was so sad to see her leave. We promised to stay in touch, but that is hard to do when you are a nomad. I don't get many letters, for instance. And we met before I even knew about cell phones, let alone had one.

That was the amazing thing about these tourists. As much as we shared our life with them, they opened up theirs to us. They connected us to the rest of the world. They taught me about different foods, places, and customs. Whereas I thought their lives sounded crazy—houses with boxes that carried you from one floor to another? Stairs that moved? Food that was wrapped in plastic and sold in stores? Milk that came in cartons? Dogs that slept in your bed? Bathrooms with showers and toilets?

These were all as foreign and strange to me as I am sure drying dung patties for fuel and hunting with eagles were for them. It was an education, for all of us.

6

Asher Arrives

Most of the visitors to Bayan-Ölgii were specifically interested in hunting with eagles. Like Asher, a photographer from Israel, which was a country I had never heard of.

I was twelve years old when Asher showed up. It was late October 2012. I was in the paddock, milking our cow, when I heard the growl of the engine growing louder. In the distance, I saw a metal rectangular box barreling toward our house, kicking up a cloud of fine, gold-colored dust in its wake.

ASHER ARRIVES

It was the familiar gray Russian van called a Furgon. I heard it idle to silence, and then my father's loud voice as he greeted the strangers. I recognized the voice of the translator, a man from Ölgii whom my dad had become friends with over the years. My dad assumed that the man he had brought with him was just another tourist who wanted to learn about the nomadic life, like the others. He welcomed them both into our home.

Asher was a big, tall guy with dark brown hair, a mustache, and a beard. He looked like a grizzly bear but had a smile that matched his laugh, which filled our home the minute my father invited him inside. He had come to Mongolia to see the Golden Eagle Festival, which has been held in Ölgii since 2000. The festival is named for the majestic bird indigenous to the steppes that nomads have been hunting with for centuries.

The history of eagle hunting in Bayan-Ölgii stretches back 2,500 years. In part, because the mountain peaks Tavan Bogd, Tsengel Khairkhan, and Tsambagarav offer safe nesting grounds and plentiful hunting for golden eagles. Eagle hunters never ate the animals that their birds caught, though. Instead, they traded fox and wolf fur for flour, cooking oil, tea, and sugar on the portion of the Silk Road (a network of ancient travel routes that connected Asia with Southeast Asia) that runs through Mongolia. This tradition was a way of life for nomads until communism outlawed eagle hunting.

The Golden Eagle Festival was founded after the fall of communism to revive eagle hunting, as the practice had dwindled as a result of the seventy-year ban. The contest was a way to bring those who had been hunting with eagles out of the shadows (like my father's family) and preserve an ancient way of our nomadic life.

In the first contest, sixty hunters participated. My father did not attend that first one, but has since competed in seventeen contests and has won three.

ASHER ARRIVES

Eagle hunters travel from all over Mongolia, but primarily from Bayan-Ölgii, to compete for the honor of best eagle hunter in all of Mongolia. Asher had come to see the festival and was so fascinated by the event that he decided to stay in the area. Before he arrived at our home, he had been traveling around to different nomad families, asking permission to photograph young eagle hunters in training. He wanted to show how the tradition was passed down from father to son. But he also wondered if there were any women or girl hunters in Mongolia.

The translator explained that every time he visited another eagle hunter, Asher would ask, "Do you know any girls or women who hunt with eagles?"

"I told him I know a girl named Aisholpan who accompanies her father on eagle hunts," the translator said. "That's why we are here."

The translator knew this because when he brought tourists to visit, I would always help my father demonstrate for them how we hunt with eagles: I would hold his eagle and he would call to her while dragging a rabbit pelt. The tourists loved that I was so comfortable with such a big bird. What the translator did not know was that I had started going on hunts as a scarer, or that I was working with my brother's eagle. That was just lucky timing.

After my father invited Asher and the translator into our home, Asher opened his backpack and pulled out a thin silver book, which I now know was a computer. We did not own one, nor did we have them at our school, so it seemed like magic to see it open up to images of the two young eagle hunters Asher had photographed already—a thirteen-year-old boy called Erkabolen and a fourteen-year-old boy named Bahkbergen, both dressed in hunting clothes, standing on hilltops with the Altai Mountains in the background, either holding or flying their eagles. Seeing the boys in those images made me feel a bit jealous. Why couldn't I do that? I knew I could be just as good as they were—maybe even better.

ASHER ARRIVES

Asher then asked my father if he could photograph me with my father's eagle, and when I heard the translation in Kazakh, I held my breath and prayed my father would say yes. I wanted to be like the boys in those photos.

Asher did not know that I was already learning how to hunt and that I had been training with my brother's eagle. That I had been studying my brother's every move since *he* began training. And that my father had been working with me in anticipation of my getting an eagle of my own.

Still, I watched my father contemplate the request. He pinned his chin to his chest and paused for what felt to me like a very long time but was probably only a few seconds.

"Aisholpan has been feeding my eagle since she was very small," my dad explained to Asher. "She takes care of her brother's eagle and already knows how to take on and off the hood, and can put the eagle on her perch. She has even been learning how to become a scarer."

I saw Asher's eyes light up. He knew enough about eagle hunting to realize that was a big deal.

"Aisholpan, do you want to do some more training tomorrow?" my father asked.

My smile was the answer. "*Jaksi!*" I said, which means "all right," or "I am good," in Kazakh. Both my mom and dad laughed. Either could have answered for me.

"This man wants to take your photo with the eagle," my dad added. "Is that fine, too?"

I smiled and nodded.

"You promise you won't cry when your picture is taken?" my dad teased in Kazakh. The translator did not need to translate into English for Asher. Neither would get the joke.

The next day, we set out in the late afternoon. Asher wanted me to wear a traditional outfit for eagle hunters, so my father pulled out Samrakhan's dark blue velvet jacket and matching pants, which had golden embroidery down the lapels and around the wrist and ankle cuffs. I slipped this on over a white turtleneck sweater and cinched my brother's thin leather belt, which is encrusted with small stones, around my waist. I then slipped on my black leather boots before placing his fox-fur hat on my head.

As I emerged from the house to join Asher and my father outside by the van, I saw my father smile.

"Jaksi," he said. "Good."

"Rakmet," I responded, and I meant it for more than the compliment.

I climbed into the back of the gray Russian van, which was already idling, with Kazakh music blaring from the radio. The twang of the stringed *dombra* melding with the growly hum of the mouth harp filled the van.

My father climbed into the front seat, holding my brother's eagle. Her hood was on and she was bobbing her head back and forth, seemingly to the beat, as we drove toward the tallest mountain nearby, roughly forty minutes away.

Asher wanted a tall peak with a dusting of snow on the ground, something that was not hard to find in Bayan-Ölgii in October. As we drove, Asher scanned the horizon and shouted and pointed when he saw a mountain peak emerge—a majestic and sprawling pyramid covered with a layer of snow that made it stand out above all the rocky hilltops that surrounded it—brown, brick red, and muted gray against a soft white backdrop.

"*Perfect!*" Asher shouted as the van sped up toward the closest hill. As usual with any driving in Bayan-Ölgii, there was no road—just hard-packed terrain that trucks, motorbikes, horses, and camels alike could traverse. Our van splashed through a lazy, meandering river and past a herd of drinking goats before coming to a halt.

I climbed out and met my father at the base of the small, rocky hill that Asher had chosen for the first photo. My father gave me the leather glove, which I slipped on my right hand, and then he placed the eagle on my arm.

I felt her weight—fourteen pounds—and she was so tall that her head rose higher than mine as she wrapped her strong talons around my wrist. She was still wearing her hood, and my father advised me to wait until I was settled in the spot where my picture would be taken before removing it, so that the eagle would remain calm.

I began climbing to the top of the hill, using my left hand to pull my body up while balancing this toddler-sized bird on my right arm, and experienced the same sense of joy I feel whenever I gallop my pony up into the mountains.

My dad climbed behind me, saying nothing but a few words of encouragement—to me and to the bird.

"You have a good way with her," he said as we made the ascent. "I can tell she trusts you."

I felt that as well.

Once we got to the spot where Asher asked me to sit, I looked down below. Asher, this big, burly guy, looked so small in the distance. He gave me the thumbs-up and then started pointing his camera lens toward me and the eagle. That was my sign to take off her hood.

Once I slipped it off her head, she looked right at me. Her eyes were pitch-black and shiny. They locked with mine, and I felt a tingling throughout my whole body. Then she turned her head from side to side in quick, deft movements, starting and stopping abruptly to take in the scene around her. Her entire body tensed, as if she were ready to launch. Long leather straps were attached to the cuffs on her feet, just above her claws, and I wrapped them around my right hand in case she wished to fly sooner than I wanted her to.

My father had a skinned rabbit leg in his bag. He clambered down the hill and got to a spot that was out of the camera's view. Once he was in place, he gave Asher the thumbs-up and then pointed at me

ASHER ARRIVES

and did the same. I stood up and held my arm out straight to one side, and then my father yelled, "Huka!"—his signal for my brother's bird to launch.

I knew that Asher wanted to document the ancient practice of eagle hunting, and how the tradition is passed on from father to child. But I had never been photographed in this formal way before. Yes, tourists took snapshots of me, my father, and my brother. But this felt different. As if both my brother's eagle and I were on a stage, not just out on a practice hunt. I think she knew this, too, because when her talons tightened around my arm this time, just before she launched into the air, her ascent felt lighter, easier, and more free than it had in the past. As she rose, she spread her wings so quickly that a shadow was cast over my face, and for a second her wings shielded me from the late-autumn sun. I watched in awe as she soared into the air and toward my dad, who was waving the skinned rabbit leg in the air. In the stillness of that chilly afternoon, I could hear the sounds of

Asher's camera—*click, click, click, click, click*—carried on the breeze and mingling with my father's *"Huka!"* call.

We did that several times, until the sun started its early descent. It was tiring, but I was too excited to notice. Asher put his camera in its bag and waved both hands in the air as if he were doing half a jumping jack. Time to come down.

I placed the eagle back on my arm, which now ached from the exertion, and held on to her tether as I made my descent.

Back at the van, Asher looked neither happy nor sad. Sort of in between.

"He did not get the shot he wanted," our translator said. "He wants to try one more location."

My father and I said that was fine, though my stomach was starting to rumble. We climbed back in the van, and I dug a piece of rock cheese from my coat pocket. We drove another half an hour, the sky turning from a bright blue to a more muted lavender with every passing minute.

ASHER ARRIVES

Asher saw another clump of hills in the distance, without the big snowy mountain in the background, and he shouted to the driver, "Let's go there!"

This time, the ascent was a breeze. My father and I had had a good practice run, and both the eagle and I had had our snacks. We were ready.

For this shot, Asher asked me to do the same thing: let the eagle fly to my father. But something changed. When I took off the eagle's hood, she looked at me for a short time. My father called her, as he had done earlier that day, but the eagle kept looking at me. She then spread her wings, which spanned six feet, and instead of springing into the air, she wrapped one wing around me and gave me a hug. The love I felt for her at that moment was so big that I forgot why we were there. Instead of encouraging her to fly, I put my cheek next to her beak and she nuzzled me, as a child does its mother.

My father's *"Huka!"* pulled me out of that magical moment.

"Huka!" We both heard it again.

She darted her head in the direction of my father's voice. With my heart, I felt her talons grip and release and watched her leap into the air, and with my eyes I followed her as she landed on my father's arm with such grace and beauty that I was overcome with emotion.

By then the sky had turned from lavender to a darker purple, with a strip of bright orange that made the pale brown-and-tan desert glow golden.

We heard Asher yell "Got it!" from below.

Perfect timing, as the sun had all but disappeared.

We walked back to the van, smiling. Both my father and I knew something magical had just happened.

7

Otto, Not Just Another Excited Tourist

That winter, I had a habit of asking my father the same question over and over: "When can I get my own eagle?"

I knew that the babies hatched in March and stayed in their nests for four months before learning to fly. My birthday was in May, and twelve or thirteen is the age when most boys traditionally start training....

Asher had been gone for months, and life had

gone back to normal. School during the week, home on the weekends, helping my parents with the goats, sheep, and cows. Still, what I looked forward to more than anything was taking care of my brother's eagle.

I was relentless. "Wasn't I supposed to get an eagle for my birthday?" became my new joke. My father never laughed. But he did nod every so often.

And then one evening, after he had been out herding the goats, he called to me as he rode his horse up to our stable. I was helping my mother with washing the clothes in a large bucket, laying the wet pants over the rock wall behind our house as he clip-clopped up to us.

"Aisholpan, I spotted it this afternoon!" he said, smiling.

"Spotted what?" I asked.

"Your eaglet!" he said as he slowed his horse to a stop and threw his leg behind him to dismount.

"Where?" I threw the wet, still-sudsy pants

onto the rocks and ran over to him. His horse was thirsty and needed a drink.

"Just a twenty-minute ride from here, by the plateau where the goats are now grazing," he said. I knew the exact spot. There was a small cliff that had a rock ledge jutting off it. The perfect place for a nest.

"I was out herding the goats when I saw the mother fly into her nest," he said excitedly. "Then I saw two eaglets with my binoculars. Now we just need to protect them from anyone else trying to steal them."

It made me think that Asher had watered the seed that I had already planted in my father's mind. I remembered that after we had finished the photo shoot that day, months before, he had asked my dad, "Would you ever let Aisholpan hunt with her own eagle?"

And my dad had answered, "We have already been discussing this."

And when tourists came to visit that summer,

my father had let me hold his eagle for a few photos. That was a first.

Scouting an eaglet for me to train was the next level. It was happening.

And then, like magic, Asher came back to see us the following week, this time with another tourist named Otto Bell. He was from Britain but lived in New York City. My dad still describes Otto as the guy with the crazy hair because it stuck up all over the place. He also ran his hands through it whenever he got excited or when he was talking, which meant his hair was always standing up because he was always talking and usually excited.

Asher showed us the photos he'd taken of me the summer before. He had them stored on his computer, but as gifts, he'd also made a few prints, which he took out and laid on the table. Otto started talking with his hands and running them through his hair. He was talking very fast, and the translator was trying to keep up.

"I fell in love with this photo," he said. He

pointed at one of the prints that Asher had brought me. It was the one in which my brother's eagle had just launched from my arm and was in midair, its wings spread as wide as my smile.

I remembered that moment.

"It tells a whole story," Otto continued. "The story of eagle hunting, of the Kazakh nomads. Of the strength of girls. Of this extraordinary life you live."

My father was nodding along, thinking this was just another excited tourist.

But then Otto said something that was different.

"I want to make a movie about eagle hunting," he said, still very excited. "And I want it to focus on Aisholpan."

"Something similar to what Asher did?" my dad asked.

Both Asher and Otto agreed: Yes, similar, but more involved.

"It would mean my living with you and your family, and filming you training Aisholpan to hunt," Otto said.

My dad smiled. He knew how much I enjoyed having my picture taken with his eagle. "We are about to steal a baby eaglet. Is this something that interests you?"

Otto's eyes went wide, and he nodded up and down many times, before he said, "Yes, that would be great!"

My father told Otto that we would take him to the nest the following day. Then he turned to me and said with a wink, "You said you wanted to be an eagle huntress, right?"

The next morning, we saddled up our ponies and packed rope and a big blanket that we would use to wrap the eaglet in once captured. We then set off for the nest. Otto followed behind us in a van. Once we arrived at the spot, my father found the eaglets with his binoculars. When I placed them to my eyes and saw two bobbing heads, my heart skipped a beat.

The eaglets were alone—their mother must have been out hunting for food, and they were still too young to fly on their own—but old enough to leave the nest. My father had timed it just so. And Otto's timing was lucky.

Before my father and I began the ascent to the top of the ridge, Otto placed a small camera on me, attached to my sweater.

"I am going to film you snatching the eagle," he explained through the translator.

I had no idea how this device worked, but it did not get in the way of my climbing, so I did not question him. I did question his enthusiasm.

I found it odd. I was excited, since this was something I had wanted to do for so long. And I knew from the dozens of tourists who had come to visit that others found eagle hunting as fascinating as I did. But I had no idea at the time that what Otto was doing would get so many others interested.

I know now that people find the idea of taking a baby eagle from its nest very strange, and perhaps even cruel, but in my culture we have such profound respect for these birds that we treat them like beloved family members. This ritual, of obtaining an eaglet from a nest before it can fly, is something my family has done for many generations. And it is not something we take lightly. There is a sacred ritual when you take a baby eagle. You must either tie a piece of white material to the nest, as a sign to other hunters that this nest has been marked, or you must drop a piece of jewelry, either a ring or an earring, into the nest. This is a way of offering something of great value—our way of giving thanks. It is purely symbolic, of course, since the mother eagle has no use for jewelry, but it is how we acknowledge just how precious we know the eaglet is, to us and to Mother Nature.

My father had a silver ring that he slipped into my pocket and said, "Leave this, so we are also offering a gift instead of just taking one."

With the ring in my pocket, my father and I started to climb.

The higher up I got, the more I started to understand how difficult it was going to be to descend to the nest, since it was on such a small ledge. The only way to get to it was by rope.

My father had brought several long lengths of thick rope, which he doubled up and then looped around my waist, tying it in a double-tight knot. He tied the other end of the rope around a rock and tugged hard on it to make sure it would hold my weight. Then he sat behind another rock and used it to steady his feet as he slowly started to let out rope, and I started my downward rappel.

I had never done anything like this before—and, I will admit, I was scared. But I would not let fear get in the way of my dream. My father coached me: "Place your foot on that crevice," he shouted. "Grab onto that stone."

I slowly made my way down the rock face, feeling the rope tighten around my waist as the cliff got steeper. My heart was now pounding so loudly that I could barely hear my dad's instructions.

Just breathe, I thought as I slowly made my way down toward the nest.

"Steady," I heard my father coach from above. "Take your time."

Just then, I placed my foot on a rock that crumbled beneath my weight, sending a shower of pebbles bouncing down and off the rock face. My heart jumped into my throat as I reached quickly for another rock to hold on to and steady my now-shaking body.

"*Ayeee!*" I said not too loudly, as I did not want to upset the eaglets. By now I was close enough that I could hear chirping, little high-pitched tweets, but still could not see them. The nest was around a sharp corner and I still had a way to go before I made it there. I kept moving slowly and methodically toward those tweets.

"I see the nest!" I shouted up to my father the moment I reached the rocky ledge. "The two eaglets are nesting side by side!"

I was so relieved to have made it that far, but then I realized that the true test was about to begin.

One eaglet was standing in the nest with its beak stretched open so wide, I could see its tongue. This one was already as large as a small dog, coming up to my knees in height and with a wingspan likely as wide as I was tall. The females are bigger than the males, so I knew immediately she was the one to take. Her gangly wings were flapping awkwardly. She was swaying back and forth, still unsteady, as she was so young. I could tell that she wanted to fly away but did not know how. Her brother was smaller—male eagles always are, which is why we like to capture the females—and stayed quiet, hunkered down in the nest, watching.

"Throw down the blanket!" I shouted to my father, who began to lower it in a bundle with another rope. I then knelt before the eaglet and pinched my right fingers together, as my father had instructed me to do, and started to make tiny circles with that hand in front of her sweet little face. The idea was to mesmerize her, and it seemed to work.

She became docile just as the blanket reached the nest. I quickly untied it, and all that movement must have panicked both birds as they hopped out of the nest, away from me, onto the ledge.

"They are getting away!" I cried up to my father.

"You must hurry, Aisholpan!" he yelled back down. "The mother is coming!"

I heard strong chirps from above and looked up to see a mature golden eagle circling in the distance, heading toward the nest.

"Use the rope!" my dad yelled. I made a lasso and was able to throw it over the head and shoulders of the female eaglet. I slowly and carefully maneuvered the rope down to her torso, beneath her wings, so as not to hurt her, and then was able to drag her back into the nest.

"I got her!" I shouted up, then unfolded the blanket and placed it over her startled head. I moved quickly, tying the blanket at the bottom once she was safely inside, before tugging on the rope and shouting, "Okay!" to my father, who gently pulled the eaglet up from her nest.

The mother eagle was now circling above me, and I knew I had to get out of there fast. But first, I had to place the ring in the nest. I grabbed it from my pocket and dropped it in, far from the baby boy eaglet, and then started my ascent, which was much easier than going down. My father hoisted me as I scrambled up the cliffside.

It was not until I was sitting next to my father that I felt I could really breathe. I made it.

"Let's see what you have here," my father said as he untied the blanket and took the eaglet out. She emerged, blinking and still stunned. He put her on his hand, prying her talons open to then wrap them around his wrist, and she just looked at him and then at me, taking it all in.

"What a fine specimen you have found, Aisholpan!" my father said. He was smiling so hard, I thought his cheeks would eclipse his eyes.

She was beautiful, with fluffy white feathers interspersed throughout her brown wings and her legs and belly, too. My father petted her head, and then I did, too.

She did not pull away.

"She already likes you," my dad said with a proud smile.

My father wrapped the blanket around her wings, keeping her head exposed so she could see as we hiked back down the hill.

"That was stupendous!" Otto said as we approached him, with a smile as wide as my father's. "I think we got all of it on film."

I was not thinking about the film or Otto or anything but my eaglet, whom I decided to call White Feathers.

She was my eagle. I had caught her. I would train her. And she was what would finally make me an eagle huntress.

8

How to Train an Eagle

We got right to work. It was summer, which meant I had all day to learn how to train my eagle. The Golden Eagle Festival takes place the first weekend in October. I told my father that I wanted to enter it that same year.

"Aisholpan!" he said. "It takes years to become an eagle hunter."

I think even he was shocked at my confidence. But I knew there was something special about my bird.

White Feathers was still a baby, so the bonding

was immediate. I fed her little cubes of rabbit or lamb meat, placing them on long skewer sticks and putting them near her beak. Watching her peck and gobble the food made me so happy. She would then rub her beak on my hand or arm, which my father said was a sign of affection.

She was still too young to fly but would be ready to take flight by August. I spent that month practicing with the hood my father made for her, putting it on and pulling it off. I also placed the leather tethers, called *balakhbau*, on her ankles so that she could get used to them as well.

My father always says that golden eagles are like humans; if you try to train them after they are grown, they don't do as well as the young ones, who are more malleable. Since we got White Feathers so young, she had to grow up trusting me. And so, my father's first lesson was about love.

"If you are gentle and calm around your eagle, if you are good to her, then she will start to love you," he explained. "Eagles have personalities, too. Some are feistier than others. Some are naturally calm."

It soon became clear that White Feathers was a lot like me. Silent, strong, and calm. She rarely got spooked or even ruffled her feathers. But when she wrapped her talons around my wrist, I could feel her strength. I knew that if she wanted to, she could break my arm.

This is why my father kept lecturing me: "Be gentle with her, and then you won't make her angry," he'd say. "An eagle's talons are so strong that it is impossible to get them to release if they don't want to. You could attach a rope to a horse to try to pull that eagle off, and you wouldn't be able to do that. It's that strong."

I practiced holding, petting, and hooding White Feathers every day. I fed her every fourth day and watched in amazement as the meat went down her throat to the top of her chest, where it would sit for a day digesting before it descended to her belly, which would puff up a little when it was full.

She got stronger and stronger every day, flapping her wings as I put her on my arm and walked around. I also practiced placing her on her saddle perch, which looked like the one we kept in our home for her, but this one was smaller and slid into a slot on the saddle to keep it upright when we were riding. She took to it naturally, with no drama at all. Calm. So calm.

It was late August when my dad could tell that she was ready to fly. It was time to train her to come to me when I called.

We saddled our ponies and took White Feathers to a hilltop not far from home. My dad had packed a rabbit skin in his bag.

"We will first teach her how to track the rabbit," he said.

He took White Feathers and instructed me to ride down the hill and drag the rabbit pelt behind me on my pony.

Once I was in the right position, he called down, "When you call her, make the sound *huu-kaa!* Eagles can feel that sound in their stomachs, almost like goose bumps. That is the hunter's signal that she should get ready to fly and catch her prey."

I had seen my father and brother do this countless times, and had even started doing it with my brother's eagle. But this was different. This was my eagle.

I gave him a thumbs-up so he knew I was ready, and then I started trotting my pony, dragging the rabbit behind me on a very long rope that I had looped around its neck.

"*Huukaa!*" I shouted, trotting in one direction and looking back at White Feathers, who was not leaving my dad's arm, just looking left and right and then back at me.

"Try again!" my dad yelled down.

I turned my pony around to go back toward my start position.

From there, I tried again, trotting a bit faster, yelling a bit louder. This time, White Feathers looked at me. My heart skipped a beat. "*Huu-kaa!*"

I shouted, making the *hu* extra-guttural and the *kaa*... stretched out and bumpy with each trot.

I looked back at White Feathers, who spread her wings and looked ready to launch. But then she decided against it and folded her wings back into her body.

This was harder than I'd imagined.

"Make your voice even more forceful, Aisholpan!" my dad yelled down from the hilltop. "That sound calls her to attention. She has to identify it as you, your sound. No one else's. Make it special!"

I took a deep breath and shouted, "*Hu-ka!*" hitting the "ka" extra hard. My dad shook his head. My bird did not budge. Then I tried elongating both the *huuuu* and the *kaaaaa*. Still nothing.

I tried one more time—strong, confident, and loud. White Feathers pricked up her head and pointed her beak toward me.

"That is it, Aisholpan!" my dad said. "I could feel in her body that she recognized you!"

I trotted back to the starting place, determined to get it this time. I threw the rabbit out behind my pony and started trotting forward, not looking back but only ahead, and mustered all my thought and focus on my call:

"HUUKAA!" I shouted, loud and strong.

And then again. "HUUKAA."

I sensed her movement before even turning my head, and when I did turn, she was soaring right at me, wings spread, beak pointed toward the rabbit, which she landed on without making a sound.

"Good, Aisholpan!" my dad yelled from the hilltop. "Good!"

We did this exercise several more times that afternoon, and each time, White Feathers got to the rabbit a little more quickly, with a little more precision.

"The sound of each hunter is different," my dad explained on our ride back home. "She knows your sound now. She is a smart bird. An excellent bird. She will make you proud."

I was already so proud, and I let her know. Every time I would go to take White Feathers off the rabbit pelt that day, I petted her neck and told her what a good bird she was, and then I rewarded her with a small piece of meat. She chirped back at me, as if to say thank you, and my father explained to me that, just as hunters have their own sounds, so do eagles.

It depends on their size, how thick or thin they are. But each one chirps differently, and a good hunter can recognize the sound of his or her bird just as the bird recognizes the sound of their hunter.

"This is very important, Aisholpan," my father explained as we were riding down the hill. "Especially at the Golden Eagle Festival, where there are sixty or seventy hunters and as many eagles. You win based on how well you know your bird and she knows you."

As he was talking, White Feathers was chirping. We were riding home, and she had her hood on, but I think she was happy and proud of how well she had done that day.

I was, too.

We kept practicing with the rabbit pelt, and I had gotten so good that when Otto came back to visit, he filmed me working with White Feathers. He could not believe how well she was doing. My father could. He kept saying, "This is a great eagle."

My dad has had eight eagles in his lifetime. We keep them for several years and then let them fly to the sky. They are not our birds. We just have the privilege to live with them.

Otto found this intriguing and was eager to understand what made an eagle great.

"The great eagles," my dad explained, "have very special eyes. Some eagles' eyes are dull—but others, you can see this flame instead of a pupil. It is so intense that you are almost afraid. It's like the sun—you can't look straight into it."

Otto was listening intently, as was I.

I went outside to check on White Feathers. She was on her perch and had her hood on. I slipped it off, curious. I had seen her eyes so many times before but had never thought of them as flames. I had never thought to look into them directly. When I did, I understood what my father meant. They did not burn me, but I did see the flicker. It was as if she were looking deep inside me. Into my past and my future.

In early September, my father felt it was time to try to catch a fox.

In the past, I was the one who would go and scare the fox, and my father would send his eagle to catch it. This time, my father wanted White Feathers to do the hunting—with me as the hunter.

HOW TO TRAIN AN EAGLE

As we rode out to a spot my father knew would be good for hunting, he began to explain how an eagle hunts.

"An eagle can see twice as well as a human, so when she is up in the air, circling, she is scanning for movement," he explained. "Sometimes the eagle circles the fox so high, the fox does not even see her. That is the eagle playing a trick. She is hovering high up, waiting. When the fox thinks it is safe, the eagle makes her move. And that is when she strikes. The best eagle hunters just let the eagle be the best hunter she already is."

I soaked up every word. It all made sense to me: I was not training my eagle. She was training me.

We arrived at the spot where my father was sure we would find foxes. He told me to go with White Feathers to the highest plateau. Once we were there, I took off her hood and moved her from the perch to my arm. I had gotten used to her weight by then. We both started to scan the horizon as my father trotted back and forth in zigzag motions, shouting and kicking up rocks and dust to scare any foxes out of hiding.

As I watched him in the distance, I heard his lessons in my head. "Whenever she is hunting a fox, a good eagle knows automatically what to do: when to fly, where to look, how to spot, and when to swoop. Foxes hide in the crevices of rocky mountains. The eagle knows to sit and wait for the hunter to make the signal."

I was waiting for the signal.

Then I saw it, a flash of silver fur scurrying across the brown-red earth. My eagle saw it, too. "*Huu-kaa!*" I shouted, and felt goose bumps all over. I could see her body tense up, poised to take flight. I watched her zoom in on the fox, and then felt the lift. This was my moment to gently push her into the air, like a springboard, as my father had instructed me.

Watching her launch into the air, her wings spread wide, was thrilling. She climbed up, up, up into the bright blue sky and began to soar and circle, searching for her target. As soon as she spotted it, she circled again, planning her attack, and then dived straight at it like a bullet shot from a gun.

I was so excited, I almost forgot that my job was to gallop down to meet her. I saw my dad already heading that way, and so I shouted, "*Hiya!*" to my pony and headed straight for White Feathers. When I arrived, she was hunched over the fox, her talons wrapped tightly around its neck and heart. Its fur was still intact. My dad was already there, waiting for me.

"The great eagle thinks more than people do sometimes," he explained. "This one is so smart, she killed the fox quickly—but she did not ruin the skin during the kill. She doesn't eat it. She is waiting for you."

When I moved closer to her, I saw her wings relax, lowering an inch. I knelt next to her and praised her while my father instructed me to get the rabbit leg out of my bag.

I grabbed the skinned leg and held it in one hand, and then I used it to lure her off the fox and onto my gloved hand.

She ate with gusto!

"She must be hungry!" I said as she tore at the purple-red meat.

"She is feeling victorious!" my father said. "She caught her first fox!"

I was feeling victorious, too. My father picked up the fox, which was half as tall as me and had the most beautiful silvery pale-orange fur.

"Your first fox, Aisholpan!" he said as he handed it to me.

I held the still-warm fox in my hands and looked up at the sky to give thanks for its sacrifice. Then I presented it back to my father.

"This is for you," I said, and bowed my head. "You have taught me well."

My father took the fox and smiled hard before he responded. "She has taught us both."

When we returned home, my mom was eager to

hear how it went. When she saw the fox pelt tied to my father's saddle, she knew we had succeeded.

We sat down to dinner and started eating the bone broth soup with dumplings she had made. After four hours of hunting, I was famished.

Between bites, I told my mother, sister, and baby brother about the hunt. Not about what I did, but about what White Feathers had done. "She was magnificent!"

"That is great!" my mother said. "Will she be ready for the festival?"

It was only several weeks away and we had one hunt thus far. We would go out a few more times before I would enter a ring surrounded by tourists and compete against the best eagle hunters in the region. But I knew that she would be ready, just as I knew she would catch that fox. I knew there was nothing for me to do but trust her. She knew how to hunt, just as my people, the Kazakhs, knew how to hunt with them.

After dinner, I went outside to say good night

to White Feathers. And to thank her—for trusting me.

She was sitting on her perch with her hood on. She turned her head toward me before I even said a word. She knew it was me.

"Nice work, White Feathers," I whispered as I took off her hood. I looked into her eyes, and they did sparkle like embers in a fire. "Rakmet."

9

Blessings and Opinions

My grandfather was one of the greatest eagle hunters in Mongolia. Getting his blessing was important.

There were eagle hunters within our community who believed girls should not hunt—that girls were not strong or talented enough. My father knew this was not the case for me. He knew I could do it. But he wanted to know how my grandfather felt, as I would be the first female eagle huntress in our family line.

My father explained this to my grandfather one day as they sat outside in the warm sun, and waited for his response. My grandfather considered this for a moment before he said, "We have been hunting with eagles from our forefathers. My father and his father were trained by their fathers. It is in our blood."

Moments later, my grandfather called to me.

I came running out of the house to see him.

He commended me on capturing White Feathers by saying, "This is a hard bird to catch!" with a teasing smile. Then he grabbed my hand and said, "May God help you pursue the hunter's path. May God keep you healthy. May you grow old with yellow teeth like me. May no bird escape your hands, and may no horse leave you on your journey. God is great. I entrust that eagle to you."

My grandfather taught my father to hunt with eagles, and now he would help train me, too.

When school started that September, I had been training White Feathers for two months. On my first day of school, I told my best friend, Aimaral, that I was going to compete in the Golden Eagle Festival at the end of the month.

Her eyes grew so wide, I thought they might pop out of her head.

"In the famous festival?" she said, surprised.

We were lying on our beds in the dormitory, catching each other up on our summers.

"Yes!" I said, laughing. "What other festival is there?"

"How is that even possible?" she asked. "Your father allowed you to do this?"

I smiled and said, "Of course!"

"And your mother?" she added. "She also said it was fine?"

I explained that my mother was harder to convince.

"She worries I will get teased," I said. "That the judges may not respect me."

"You are strong, Aisholpan!" Aimaral said. "You will do well."

A few other girls came into the dorm, and Aimaral announced, "Aisholpan is going to compete in the eagle-hunting contest!"

There was a gasp followed by so many animated questions.

"Is that in the rules?" one girl asked.

It was a good question, and I did not know the answer. Were there rules for entering the contest? If so, I had no idea what they were. I just knew I was going to Ölgii to compete. And I could not wait! My girlfriends were so supportive.

"If any girl can do it, it is you, Aisholpan!" Aimaral said.

Everyone in my dorm agreed, including Saigulikh, who was the only girl there who knew how special White Feathers was.

"If any eagle can do it, it is White Feathers!" she added.

Word got around school that I was competing, and the boys had a very different response. They all laughed, but not in a nice way.

BLESSINGS AND OPINIONS

"Girls should stay home," one boy said.

"Girls can't eagle-hunt," another said. "You will be too scared! Eagles are too fierce."

"You don't have the stamina," another chimed in. They were all laughing, and my face began to burn red hot. Not because I was embarrassed, but because I was determined to prove them wrong.

"Just you wait," I said. "I will show you!"

Their teasing only made me that much more determined.

10

The Road to Ölgii

It takes six hours to make it to Ölgii on horseback, and eight if you are traveling with an eagle, as you have to make multiple stops to let them rest. My father and I woke up early the morning before the contest in order to make the long trek. I ate breakfast quickly and began getting dressed. My mother was staying behind with Saigulikh and Dinka. She braided my hair that morning into two long plaits, clasped at each end with white lace flowers, before placing my brother's eagle hunting hat on me—its fox-fur brim fanned above my face.

The morning we left for Ölgii, Samrakhan called to wish me luck.

My brother knew I was competing. He also knew that I had caught my own eagle. He was still in the army but called every week to touch base. My dad assured him that I was still looking after his eagle, and that I would be more willing to give his eagle back now that I had my own to train.

"You are lucky I am not competing, too," he said that morning. "Now you actually have a chance to win!"

I laughed at him and said, "I just hope my eagle can find me!"

I had never been to the festival before but had heard so many stories from my father, a veteran. He said that the biggest challenge was to have your eagle hear *your* voice in the crowd, as there would be so many hunters and eagles at the event. It was hard enough for older, better-trained eagles to handle that level of distraction, but even harder for young eagles, like White Feathers, who had never been with more than six or seven people at a time. There would be a hundred people at least!

I had heard that some eagles get so confused that they fly to the wrong person or just fly off, away from the crowds, because they are not used to so many people.

White Feathers was still a baby. She had only just learned to fly that same summer, with me. We would both be the youngest girls at the contest!

My mother sensed my nervousness as she secured the thin leather beneath my chin, and asked, "How does that feel?"

I nodded my head, fine.

My father dressed in his wolf coat. Even though he would not compete that year and was going solely as my coach and support, he wanted everyone to know that he was a great hunter. Both for the competition itself and in regular life, eagle hunters are judged by their outfits, and you can always tell how successful an eagle hunter is by his coat, pants, and hat: To have an entire suit made of wolf meant your eagle has killed an animal three times as big, and ferocious, as a fox. It is the sign of a truly great eagle—and hunter.

We saddled our ponies, placed our eagles on their leaning sticks, and began the journey to Ölgii. My father knew the way instinctively. He did not need to follow the tracks that had carved a faint road into the tundra. He used the position of the sun in the sky, the curve of a river, and the shape of a mountain peak to find his way. It was a long ride, and White Feathers sat patiently on her stick, chirping every once in a while as I spoke to her in soothing ways, giving her—and myself—a pep talk.

"Tomorrow, there will be lots of eagles in the competition. You must ignore them, and focus on me," I said as we rode. She had her hood on, but when I spoke, she turned her head toward me, as if listening to my every word.

"Remember my voice," I continued. "This is the most important thing to do. When I call, you come to me. Ignore the other hunters and noises from the crowd. They will be a distraction if we let them."

It is one thing to have your eagle fly to you quickly and land on your arm when you are on a quiet, familiar hillside with no one watching. It is another thing entirely when you are surrounded by fifty or more eagles and eagle hunters and performing in front of a crowd of hundreds of tourists with clicking cameras. I had no idea what that would feel like. I just knew we would both have to focus.

It was the last weekend in September and the weather was cool but sunny. The horses had worked up a sweat, and I had as well.

I knew we were getting close when I saw the smoke streams in the air. We had passed only four nomadic homes during our trip, but as we got closer to the city, we started to see more homes, closer together, which meant more heating and cooking stoves emitting curlicues of smoke. People who lived in Ölgii lived in permanent houses, made of concrete or wood. They had animals, but not herds of hundreds, like the nomads throughout the province.

Soon the packed dirt became a paved road beneath my horse's hooves, which meant the clopping had a more distinct sound. White Feathers had never heard or felt this before. She suddenly became more alert, bobbing her head up and down.

Ölgii has streets and stop lights, and stores that sell food and clothes and gas and more. I had been there only a few times before, and it was always a treat. We went directly to my father's brother's home, which was on the outskirts of town. After we tied up our horses in his backyard and fed them and our eagles, my father and I went into town, leaving our animals behind to rest after the long journey.

I loved walking past all these shops and grocery stores. We had nothing like this in Altansogts, where I went to school. This was the big city, and though there were other nomadic country people walking through the streets, I stood out in my embroidered pants and fox-fur hat. Most people in the city wore Western clothes—jeans, sweaters, and parkas. All these items were available for sale at the department store, which was where I wanted to go. Seeing all of the fashionable clothes and fancy things people could buy—from hair barrettes to high-heel shoes to face cream that smelled sweet like flowers, not sour like the yak butter we rub on our face when the weather gets really cold and dry—was all so fascinating.

That night, we ate a good dinner that tasted that much more delicious after the long ride. Both my father and uncle were giving me advice—too much advice! My head was swimming.

"When you get to the festival, ignore anyone who says anything to you," my uncle said. "The other hunters will make fun of you because you are a girl. Do not let them intimidate you!"

"Keep focused on your eagle," my father added. "She will feel your nervousness, and that will interfere with her performance. This is all about staying calm—and she will stay calm, too."

"And make sure that when you ride in front of the judges, you are really alert! Sit up straight and hold White Feathers up for all to see! This is a time to shine." My uncle was on a tear.

The effects of a full belly and the long ride were starting to overcome any nervousness I may have had. My eyelids felt so heavy, it was hard to keep them open. I began to nod my head, first agreeing with my dad and uncle, and then just falling asleep! My body all of a sudden felt weighed down by heavy rocks. I said good night to everyone and then walked outside to check on White Feathers, who was resting on her perch. I knew she was a bit hungry—she chirped at me to say so—but I also knew she needed to be a bit hungry for the contest.

"You will eat well tomorrow!" I whispered as I petted her head and neck. She chirped at me. "A feast! I promise."

11

The Golden Eagle Festival

"Today is the big day!" the radio blasted through the one-room house the next morning. "The day of the Golden Eagle Festival, when hunters from all over Bayan-Ölgii will come to compete!"

"Let's go!" I kept urging my dad, who was taking his time over tea.

"What's your rush?" he joked.

Finally, we got our birds, mounted our ponies, and started our trek to the festival site on the outskirts of town. I had heard so much about the legendary Sayat Tobe, Hunter's Hill, that I gasped when I finally saw it rise up from the flatlands. I understood why it was so famous. It stood out in the midst of a huge flatland, offering the perfect launchpad, with many nooks, crannies, and ledges from which to perch and fly eagles.

As we approached, we saw eagle hunters on their ponies converging from every direction—north, south, east, and west—carrying their eagles. Some people arrived on camels decorated with colorful fabric saddles, and so many others came in cars, on motorbikes, or piled into vans.

It was easy to tell the hunters from the tourists: Those who were competing wore ornately embroidered suits, like mine, or ones fully made of fox or wolf fur, like my father's.

Participants register on the day of the contest, so no one knew I was coming. My father had not told anyone but close family that I was competing. From a distance, people may have mistaken me for a boy, as I was dressed in the traditional outfit of a young hunter. But as I got closer to the grounds and passed several hunters, I saw their heads snap my way, confused. My long braids, fastened with white lace flower barrettes at the ends, were the giveaway.

Once we arrived at the festival grounds, I lined up with the other competitors and my father to sign in.

"What is she doing here?" an elder hunter asked my father.

"That is my daughter Aisholpan," he said proudly. "She is competing today."

One man laughed so hard that a few turned to see why, and he nodded toward me. This caused others to laugh as well. I felt my cheeks burn. I decided to ignore them and instead whispered to White Feathers, "Forget them. Focus on me."

This was my mantra as I made my way toward the judges' table to sign in.

There were five judges, including the governor of Ölgii and the head of the Eagle Hunter Society.

"Name?" one of the judges asked without looking up.

"Aisholpan," my father said.

The judge looked up.

"A girl?" he said.

The other judges looked as well.

Each one seemed stunned.

Another judge said, "A young girl."

"Yes," my father said.

There was more laughter from the crowd circling the judges' table, as well as from the other hunters lined up behind me. I tried to ignore it. There was no rule that a girl could not compete—we had checked—but for a moment I wondered if they would allow me to enter.

Then I watched with relief as the judge wrote my name in the registration book and handed my father my number. I would be the twenty-fourth of seventy eagle hunters who would compete that day. Having that ticket and my place gave me a sense of relief. I wanted to compete because I love eagle hunting. I love being a nomad girl. I love being in the mountains. If boys could compete, why not a girl? I knew I was just as good as they were. Today was my day to prove it.

When it was time, I ignored the stares and laughs, and followed my father to line up with the rest of the contestants for the first competition: outfit, appearance, and riding style.

I took my place in the line of seventy hunters and waited for my name to be called. At that moment, you must ride your horse, holding your eagle, in front of the judges. They give you scores of one to ten based on your outfit, horse, and equipment: the saddle, reins, and eagle-hunting gear, which includes the leaning stick and the small embroidered leather bag worn around the waist to carry the rabbit leg for your eagle.

As the hunters before me were called, one by

one, to parade in front of the judges, my father looked me over one last time and said, "You must sit up tall and look your best!"

He was on his horse next to me on mine. White Feathers was very calmly sitting on my arm, which was resting on the leaning stick. Beneath my coat, I could feel my heart pounding.

Another hunter was called, and my father reached over to straighten my hat. He was nervous, too. I could see his hands shake ever so slightly as he refastened my chin strap.

Just then, my name was called.

Word had gotten around that a girl had registered. As I started walking my horse out from the line of hunters and toward the judges' table, I heard someone shout, "Congratulations!"

Another shouted, "Good luck!"

But others in the crowd laughed. I tried to block them out. When I finished parading in front of the judges, I heard someone say, "Oh, that is the girl we heard about. Look how young she is. She can't be an eagle hunter!"

Those words hurt me a bit, but I am not someone who cries when someone says something mean. Instead, those words gave me strength and inspiration to do my best.

I was relieved to get good scores for my outfit and equipment—two eights and two tens. Not four tens, like the son of a famous eagle hunter from Altai who went before me. But good enough.

From there, my dad and I made our ascent up Sayat Tobe to find a spot and wait my turn. Not only was I the only girl, I was also the youngest participant, but there were other young men there with their fathers and grandfathers as well. Some of the older men were there to compete as well as to coach their family members.

I got off my pony and sat down on the hillside with my eagle and studied my competition and their birds. I had been practicing so hard during the prior months, but this was my first time doing this with hunters other than my dad.

I was so relieved that I was the twenty-fourth person to compete. That meant I could study their moves and take notes.

The next event was to drag a fox skin behind your horse and call your eagle, as my father had taught me earlier that summer. The judges time how quickly the eagle is able to land on the fox. I knew White Feathers could do this easily. I just had to concentrate on calling her. That meant my voice had to penetrate the din from the chirping eagles and the audience that had formed in a large circle around the arena.

"When you perform for the first time, you get nervous," my father explained to me as we watched the first dozen hunters compete. The older hunters had no problem—their eagles went straight to them. The younger hunters struggled a bit more. One eagle got so distracted that, instead of flying down into the arena, she took a hard left and flew over to another hunter waiting his turn. The whole audience gasped and then laughed. Another eagle started off well, but then totally missed the fox and instead flew over the crowd before circling back and disappearing behind Sayat Tobe. More laughter rose from the crowd as the hunter galloped after his errant eagle.

Watching those eagles that landed on the fox pelt, as they were supposed to, made my heart soar. It was so beautiful to watch. I knew White Feathers could do this but worried she might get frightened by the crowd of six hundred people surrounding the arena below.

My turn was coming up soon, so my father told me to go down to get my pony ready.

"You must ride with confidence, Aisholpan," he explained before I went. "Your pony can also get nervous and run into the crowd, so if you stay calm, the pony and the eagle will, too. Show them who is boss."

When I heard my name called through the loudspeaker, I knew that was my signal: time to compete. I trotted into the arena and the crowd got quiet. I looked behind me and saw my father and White Feathers at the top of Sayat Tobe. My father shouted down, "Use your voice, Aisholpan!"

That was my cue. I started to canter my pony down the middle of the arena and shouted, "HUU-KAAA!" as loudly as I could. I turned back and saw White Feathers launch, and my heart launched with her.

"*Huukaaa!*" I shouted again and again, careful to keep my pony cantering in a straight line, not zigzagging, dragging the fox pelt behind me, and giving White Feathers enough space around me to make an easy, wide-open landing.

The audience was watching with bated breath, I could tell. No one was shouting, as I had worried, but instead people had their necks craned and their eyes glued to the sky. I looked back, wondering what was taking so long, just as White Feathers made her nosedive. This was our moment: I grabbed the reins and continued my canter and could feel my eagle land with a pow, followed by a tug on the rope. That was my signal to slow my pony to a trot and then walk. The entire crowd burst into applause and cheers.

White Feathers did it! She landed on the fox, and in excellent time. I was so proud of her, I had to fight back tears.

I looked at her, standing proudly on that fox pelt, then over at the judges, who already were flashing their score cards. The first ten took my breath away. Then the second. And the third. Three perfect scores. When the fourth and fifth judges flashed their final marks, both ten, the crowd went wild again. I went to pry White Feathers off the pelt and placed her on my glove.

"We did it!" I said to her as I slipped her hood back over her eyes.

My father arrived, huffing after sprinting down the hill, "That was awesome, Aisholpan!" he said. The smile on his face was bigger than any I had ever seen. "You showed them!"

Elated, we went to go have lunch and to give White Feathers some food as well. We were all famished. As I sat with other hunters inside the lunch tent, I noticed I was the only girl at the table eating. All of the other women were cooking, preparing tea, serving food to the hunters—and to me. My father was boasting, "Did you see Aisholpan out there? Did you see her eagle fly straight to that fox?"

The men around the table remained stony-faced and silent. One or two nodded. Another said, "Not all people who keep birds at home are eagle hunters."

A few other of the older men nodded in agreement.

"Her bird flew well," my father said. "She is a great eagle."

"There are many great eagles here today," another hunter said.

"Women should not be eagle hunters," one of the elder hunters added, scowling at me. "They should stay at home."

I rolled my eyes, listening to these men. Even

THE GOLDEN EAGLE FESTIVAL

after I had performed well in the morning, they were not taking me seriously. My father winked at me, as if to say, *Ignore them, Aisholpan*. I took another bite of fried bread and said nothing. I had to stay focused. The most important event—eagle calling—was coming up, and I could not let myself get distracted.

The sign of great hunters is how well they call to their eagle. My father and I had practiced eagle calling many times over, and both of us were happy with how quickly White Feathers came to my arm.

I did not feed her too much after she landed the pelt—I wanted to reward her but also to have her stay a little hungry for this next test.

The day had turned overcast and a bit cloudy. It was colder, which is better for both the hunter and bird, because if the sun is too bright, it can be blinding, and if it is too warm, the bird can be more sluggish. We went back up to the hill to wait for our turn.

I watched in awe as the hunters called their

eagles, one after another. Once again, there were several who flew in the wrong direction. One landed on the rump of a horse, who bucked. Everyone laughed. My lungs tightened at the thought. I needed to show the doubters that not only was I good enough to be an eagle hunter, but that I had the potential to be a great one.

I counted the hunters: twenty, twenty-one, twenty-two. My chest was getting tighter as my number got closer. When twenty-three mounted his horse, my dad called out, "Aisholpan! You are next!"

Before handing my father White Feathers, I said a tiny prayer that she would come quickly and deftly. And then I promised her she could eat the whole rabbit leg this time.

With that, I took another deep breath and descended the hill with my pony.

I could feel my hands trembling. I stood next to another hunter, who was probably eighteen or nineteen.

"You are up after the old man," he said.

THE GOLDEN EAGLE FESTIVAL

The eighty-year-old man who was in the ring was the oldest eagle hunter at the contest. I had heard that there were only four hundred eagle hunters left in the world—seventy of whom were competing today. I realized that I am part of a very special tribe of people—not the Tolek tribe, but of all the tribes that hunt with these majestic birds. The trembling lessened as I reflected on this, and then I quietly practiced my call to myself, not too loud so as not to confuse White Feathers, who was making her way up the hill with my father.

As I breathed in, I said, "HU," and as I breathed out, I said, "KA!"

At that moment, my name was called.

I trotted out to the center ring and waited for the pale blue flag to be lowered.

What happened next feels more like a dream.

I saw the blue flash and then felt a fire erupting in my belly that shot through my body and out my mouth: "HUKAAA!"

My pony started to gallop into the arena. I

called to White Feathers again and suddenly felt a thud on my arm.

White Feathers had landed.

My whole body felt electrified. I had no idea how long it took. I just remember hearing a small roar that grew louder as I blinked my eyes at White Feathers, who was hungrily tearing at the rabbit leg in my hand. I looked around and saw the entire crowd cheering, jumping up and down, and clapping—for me.

The judges all looked stunned.

Then one announced on the loudspeaker: "Aisholpan's bird landed in five seconds—this is the fastest an eagle has ever done this in the history of the festival. She has broken the record!"

The audience roared even louder.

The old man who went right before me, who I realized had been the one who scowled at me during lunch, came over and gave me a kiss on the cheek.

"Congratulations," he said.

He had tears in his eyes. So did I.

And then I heard my father. "AISHOLPAN!" he was yelling, running toward me, arms outstretched. "You did it!" he said.

My whole body began to shake—not from nerves or fear but from pride and joy. I quickly put White Feathers's hood back on, worried my emotions might overwhelm her. It was perfect timing, as we were both suddenly swarmed by people with cameras. Everyone wanted a picture of me and White Feathers and my proud father.

In those pictures, I know that both my eyes and his are glistening with happy tears.

There were still many eagle hunters to go, and I was elated but exhausted from the excitement. My father and I went to get a snack, and some rest, before the end of the contest. I had also promised White Feathers the entire rabbit leg. We found a place for her to eat in quiet, away from the crowd.

There were still quite a few non-eagle-hunting events before they announced the winners. I never thought I would be in the running, but my scores were so high, and White Feathers's speed so fast, there was a chance I might win a prize.

That afternoon, they did the camel race and then the Kazakh game called *tiyn teru*, a race in which one picks up a coin on the ground while on horseback. I watched *kyz kuar*, or "girl chase," which is a game in which a man chases a woman, each on his and her own horse. She has a whip that she uses to beat off the man as he chases her on his horse and tries to kiss her. If I had not been competing in the eagle hunting itself, I would have signed up for that contest. I knew I could beat off any boy from kissing me! I could also ride faster and stronger than any boy I had ever met. But when I mentioned this to my father, he shook his head at me. He did not approve. "You are too young," he said. For kissing! But not for eagle hunting.

Once all the events were done, the judges asked the contestants to line up in front of the judges' stand for the award presentation. There are prizes for the

THE GOLDEN EAGLE FESTIVAL

top three eagle hunters, each one coming with a medal and a cash prize.

The third prize was called first. It went to Nurbolat Tanu, the son of one of the best eagle hunters in the region. The second prize went to Orazkhan, another great hunter, and one of the oldest competing in the festival. He was so well known, the judges called him only by his first name, as everyone knew exactly who he was.

With each name called, my hopes were dashed. I thought that with my record-breaking time I might have had a chance at third place. Or even second. So, when it came time to announce the first-prize winner, I gave up any hope and began to mentally prepare myself to go home without a medal. I told myself, *It's okay, I did not come to win! I'm here to show myself, and White Feathers. To prove that I am an eagle huntress.*

Then I heard the judge shout through the speaker system: "And the first prize goes to . . . Aisholpan!"

The crowd erupted into applause and cheers,

and that shocked me out of my stupor—that was me! I had won! Like Orazkhan, the judges needed only say my first name, as I was the only girl competing. And by then, everyone at the festival at least knew my name.

I started trembling again as I rode my pony up to the judges' table, White Feathers on my arm, and bent my head down while the governor of Ölgii placed the medal around my neck. White Feathers was chirping in my ear, her weight feeling lighter somehow. She knew.

Another judge handed me the golden trophy that comes with first prize. Sitting on my pony, I raised the trophy in the air in celebration as the crowd continued to cheer and the judges continued to congratulate me.

"May your offspring be like her!" I heard boom through the loudspeakers just as my father arrived by my side, eyes wet with proud tears.

12

How to Catch a Fox in the Winter

The rest of that day, and the days that followed, are still hazy and dreamlike. I remember being swarmed by photographers and tourists alike. The Hollywood actress Michelle Rodriguez was there. She wanted to get her picture taken with me. Otto was there as well and had captured everything on film.

My grandfather was there, too, and he was so

proud of me. When I saw him after the award was announced, he, too, had tears in his eyes.

"Very good, Aisholpan," he said in his understated way. "Very good."

Once we got back to my uncle's house in Ölgii that evening, we called my brother.

"You have to thank me, Aisholpan!" he joked on the phone. "If I did not ask you to take care of my eagle, this may have never happened!"

That may have been true, but I could also argue that I have to thank Asher for taking my photo, my dad for agreeing to train me, Otto for wanting to make a movie, and my mom for saying yes to it all! Or I could just thank White Feathers for trusting me. In the end, she was the one creature who deserved all my thanks and respect—and I told my brother as much on the phone.

He agreed but added, "Don't forget about my eagle now that you are famous!"

We both laughed and I promised him I would never forget his eagle!

HOW TO CATCH A FOX IN THE WINTER

By the time I returned home, the news of my historic win was all over the radio and in the local and national newspapers, too. It was a big deal!

But there were naysayers as well. We started hearing the rumors almost immediately: People thought I won because I was a girl. Or that the judges gave me the prize as a publicity stunt. A lot of newspapers and magazines did write about it, but anyone who saw my eagle fly that day knew it was real. You can't fake an eagle flying to your arm in five seconds!

But then some of the older hunters insisted that no one should call me a real eagle hunter. To get that distinction, you have to catch a fox in the dead of winter in the Altai Mountains. They said, "If she is truly an eagle huntress, and this was not just a fluke, her eagle must catch a fox in the winter."

I understood that what I had already achieved

was important. Not only was I a girl who was eagle hunting but I also had broken the record for all eagle hunters, young and old. My win would have a ripple effect. I knew that, and that was all the more reason why I wanted to do the winter hunt as soon as possible. To prove to people that it was for real—that White Feathers and I were for real.

I told my father I wanted to do this. I wanted to prove to them, and myself, that I could.

Otto was still with our family when we made that decision. He had captured everything on film thus far and wanted to film the winter hunt as well.

"So, when do we go?" he wanted to know.

"January," my father said.

"I'll make sure to be here with my camera crew," Otto said. My father agreed that Otto and his two cameramen could come back to record this rite of passage.

"I just hope you can handle the cold!" my dad said, laughing.

HOW TO CATCH A FOX IN THE WINTER

I was not worried about the cold—I was used to the frigid temperatures. But I did wonder if White Feathers could catch a fox in the Altai Mountains. She was still a baby, and this was the real and true test of both the eagle and the hunter.

First, we had to prepare our horses. Trekking into the mountains in winter meant slippery snow and icy slopes. It meant sometimes wading through layers of snow that were three or four feet deep.

"Iron shoes help with the grip," my father explained as he hammered the semicircular flattened rod onto my pony's hooves.

We set out for the Altai Mountains and had already arranged to stay with my father's friend Dalaikhan, who lived on the perimeter. As we began our three-day, over-ninety-mile journey, my father warned me it would be a kind of cold like none I had never experienced before. And, just as it would be my first hunt in the mountains, it would also be my first time to the Altai Mountains in winter. I had spent summer months there, but this was markedly different. In this kind of cold, my father said, if you spit, it would freeze before it hit the ground.

My father and Dalaikhan were good friends—he had offered his home as our base for the hunt. Otto and his crew would stay with Dalaikhan's friend, who lived in the same village.

I was exhausted and went straight to bed after dinner. But I was still able to hear my father and Dalaikhan talking about the difficult conditions that we would face in the morning.

"This is an extreme cold that even we are not used to," I overheard Dalaikhan say. "It will be challenging for you—as well as your daughter and her eaglet."

White Feathers was inside with me. If we had left her outside in cold weather like this, she would have frozen to death.

The next morning, we woke up early and got dressed. I wore my tracksuit beneath a down parka, and then my cowhide pants and a black fur jacket over that.

As I walked out into the frigid morning air, the sun was just beginning to cast its pale glow over the mountains. My breath formed a halo of vapor around me, and White Feathers emitted little puffs with each chirp.

My father rode with us up into the mountains, side by side, holding his eagle as I held mine. They would show me and White Feathers how to do this. That is the rite of passage of any eagle hunter. There is an old saying in Kazakh: "What the baby sees in the nest, it then repeats when it grows up."

I had watched my father go out in the dead of winter to hunt with his eagle. I saw the look of pride on his face when he returned home with the animals he had caught. And now he was wearing those pelts in his coat, which I knew kept him warmer than the parka that Otto and his two cameramen were wearing. This was the cycle of life for the hunter. This was also something I had witnessed my entire life. As we made our way across the snow-dusted steppes toward the totally white-capped mountains, I felt connected to that cycle. As a Kazakh. As a nomad. As an eagle huntress.

"The first snow of the season is called *kahnosar*," my dad was explaining to me as we made our way. The ground beneath us shifted from snow-covered grassland to completely frozen tundra, and I felt my horse's hooves slip out from under him, even with the iron shoes on, as we made our way across what looked like a lake that had frozen a dusty blue that matched the sky.

Otto followed behind us with a translator and cameramen, stopping every once in a while to film.

"Be careful, Aisholpan," my father was coaching me as we made our way up a particularly rocky ascent that had been layered with a sheet of ice. "Horses have fallen off these icy cliffs before. We must take extreme caution."

As my pony slowly scrambled up the slippery

hill, it felt as if my fingers were being pricked by sharp, tiny daggers. At least I could feel them. My cheeks and nose were numb. Even my father complained.

"This is the coldest winter I have ever felt," he said to me more than once.

It was so cold that the camera batteries kept freezing. They had to stop filming twice that day to defrost the cameras over the warmth of the car engine.

I never complained. I was determined to catch a fox—not for Otto or for the film. For myself, for my father, for my grandfather, and for all the eagle hunters that had come before them. For Dauit. And Bulanby. And Bosaga. I also wanted to catch a fox to prove those eagle hunters wrong who said girls can't do it. That they can't handle the cold. That it is too dangerous. I would show them that they were wrong.

There were many moments when I questioned my own stubbornness, truthfully. Like when we finally made it to the top of that ridge. With those perilous cliffs behind us, I felt huge relief when I saw the pristine fluffy snow that spread out in a field in front of me. I wanted to gallop. As soon as I gave my pony a small kick to get going, she bucked a little, as if she knew what lay ahead. I urged her forward, against her will, and then felt her start to sink. She started to panic, and so did I. The snow was up to her knees, then to her shoulder, as she fought hard to scramble back to firmer ground. But there was none. My father saw what was happening and shouted, "Jump off her!"

I did and fell waist deep in the soft snow, holding White Feathers up high and grabbing my pony's reins with my free hand to slowly coax her backward, out the same way she had sunk in. Even White Feathers seemed worried. Her chirps grew more frequent and more high-pitched as I struggled to get my pony back on solid footing. Once I did, we continued to a flat, open basin, surrounded by some low-slung rocky outcrops perfect for fox dens. My dad told me to go to the highest vantage point as he rode his horse down, zigzagging and shouting, trying to scare any potential foxes out of their dens.

It worked.

I immediately spotted the pale orange-brown creature outlined by the pristine snow. My heart started racing as I took White Feathers's hood off and gave her the command. She shot up and circled before seeing the fox, but then seemed to hesitate. I don't know if she got nervous or too cold, but in that hesitation, I realized, maybe she couldn't do it.

I heard my dad yelling, which reminded me to urge her on.

"Huu-kaa!" I yelled as I started cantering toward her. It was stunning to watch her reengage with the fox and then prepare for her attack. As she zoomed in, the fox turned and stood on two back legs, in attack mode. White Feathers shifted her body suddenly from a nosedive—beak forward, wings tucked into her body—to a thrust with her feet in front of her, so that her talons were extended toward the fox. She landed one claw on its face, her talons slicing through its mouth, which left a bloody trail in the snow. At that moment, its teeth sunk into her thigh. This must have startled her, as she let go of the fox and landed about five feet away, standing there, stunned, as the fox ran off, its face bloodied.

All the air left my body. My first worry was that White Feathers had been badly hurt! I had been so focused on becoming a huntress, I forgot that she was just a baby. Not yet one year old. Was I expecting too much from her? Why else would she stop fighting? Maybe she was not such a great eagle, after all? Maybe it was really just by luck that we had won the contest.

My father had ridden up next me. "The fox is a very sly animal, not wanting to give up its life." I knew he was trying to make me feel better. But as I scanned the horizon, breathing deeply so as not to cry, I saw how many mountain peaks surrounded us. It felt endless. I could not help but feel a bit hopeless.

"So many mountains!" I said. "The fox could be hiding in any one!"

"Your eagle is still a baby, Aisholpan," my father said. "But she has talent. She just needs her moment. She will get the next one."

I felt a mix of emotions—disappointed that the fox got away and worried that White Feathers was hurt. As I put her hood back on, I asked, "Were you scared, my dear? Is it too hard to hunt so far away from home?"

My father overheard me and said, "Even the greatest eagles make mistakes, Aisholpan."

We started heading back to Dalaikhan's house as the winter sun was already beginning to set.

"Tomorrow, we will find another fox," my dad said as we rode toward the village. "And White

Feathers will catch it this time. She will know, *If I come like this, the fox is going to jump over and I need to come from this way.* She's learning."

I kept quiet, hoping what he said was true.

The next day was more of the same: We spotted one fox, but White Feathers did not even try to attack it. She just circled once or twice and then came back to me. She seemed sluggish, and I was starting to think it was too cold for her. Dalaikhan had mentioned the night before that this could be why she was struggling.

We had many more days like this. But I couldn't give up. I wouldn't.

I kept going out into the mountains with White Feathers. And Otto and his team kept coming, too. A few days became a week, became another week... until finally, one day, we set out again to another part of the mountain range and were several hours in when we saw fresh fox tracks in the snow.

"Go to the mountaintop there," my father said. "I will see if I can scare it out from hiding."

I galloped to the top and waited for my father's call.

"Hooda! Hooda!" he began to shout.

I quickly slipped White Feathers's hood off, just as I spotted the fox.

The frigid artic air carried my voice, which propelled White Feathers up into the sky.

I held my breath as I watched her scan the tundra. In a flash, she spotted the fox and started her attack, wings spread, beak pointed, like a bow and arrow, aimed right toward the fox. She swooped so close that the fox jumped to one side just as her wing grazed his back. Once again, White Feathers paused, as did my heart. In that instant, the fox dashed away.

I was ready to give up.

But then I heard my father shout, "Hooda!"

I saw the fox dash across a nearby ridge and shouted, "HUKA!"

White Feathers leaped into flight, and this time she went straight for the fox. She struck with both feet first, just as the fox also sprang back on its hind legs. What followed was wrestling and gnashing, fox versus eagle. The fox bit her, which spurred White Feathers to go in for the final kill, with one claw on its neck and the other on its heart.

As I galloped toward her, I could see her hovering over it, using all her power to squeeze.

By the time I got to her side, the fox was dead, and I was fighting back proud tears.

"Good girl," I said as I pried her talons off the fox. "You did it. You did not disappoint. I should have never questioned you."

My father had arrived by then. "I am proud of you, Aisholpan," he said. "You are the eagle huntress I always knew you would become."

13

Famous in Mongolia—and Beyond

Otto flew back to the United States from Ölgii and promised to be in touch when the film was done. He had no idea when that would be, so my father and I put it out of our minds. We were happy to return to our normal life. I did not know then that there was no returning to the life I had known before.

Word had traveled fast throughout Bayan-Ölgii and greater Mongolia that I was the girl who had won the Golden Eagle Festival. I was in newspaper and magazine articles, and as a result, not long after I'd won the contest, several private schools in Ölgii offered me scholarships to come study with them. I even got invited to go to Dubai to attend a falcon contest where falconers from all over the world come to compete.

That was in December, one month before I set out on the winter hunt with my father and a camera crew. It was a busy time for me and White Feathers. She did not come with me to Dubai, but my parents did. That was my first time ever on an airplane—theirs, too. We all prefer our feet on the ground.

But it was on that flight, as we left the ground, that I remember looking down over the shrinking landscape from my perch in the sky and wondering, *Is this how White Feathers sees the world?* Snow-blanketed mountains for miles; vast, uninhabited, white-rippled terrains as far as I could see. Eventually, no tire tracks or even road to be seen.

I returned and chose a school. My father had heard that the Turkish school offered an excellent education—and a full scholarship. Plus, I knew two other girls from Altansogts who went there. I would at least have two friends.

Everything was so different—the school was much bigger and the kids were a mix of Mongolian, Chinese, Turkish, and some Kazakh, too, but not many nomads or rural country people. I showed up in my best country clothes—jeans, a sweater, boots, and my hair braided and tied with lace bows. But I was the only person dressed that way. All the girls in that school were wearing dark skirts that reached their ankles and long-sleeved yellow-and-black tunic tops. At first, I thought, *Wow, so many teachers!*

The next day, I was given my own uniform. I was stunned—I rarely wore a skirt and found it very uncomfortable. How do you walk? Or run?

Forget about riding a horse or wrestling. It was torture. The other kids did not seem to mind. Several were chosen by the teachers to sit in the hallways and monitor people, saying things like, "No running in school," or asking for hallway passes. I was amazed! I was too shy to talk to anyone, let alone boss people around.

That was the main difference between me and most of the kids who went to this school, who were mostly rich city kids. Countryside girls and boys are very different from city kids, even now. It was a shock to me. The city kids were so mean. They made fun of the country kids—about the way we dressed and smelled. They made animal jokes and thought we were not as smart as they were.

That first day was really overwhelming, and I was so grateful when a Mongolian girl named Norov asked me to sit next to her. She taught me how to say different things in Turkish, such as *dormitory*, *teacher*, *food*, *school*, and *hi*.

I lived in the dormitory with Norov and the two girls from Altansogts. But there were other girls in our room who were not so nice to me. One in particular was quite mean. She especially made fun of the way I wore my hair, in long braids, and said that was how old ladies wore their hair. She teased me about the way I spoke, too. And about my clothes. I tried to ignore her, but one day, I'd finally had enough. I told her to stop saying mean things, and she pretended to be upset. She even said, "But your hair is so beautiful. Let me help you style it!" I fell for her trick. I sat down in front of her, and she started combing my hair. I had been in the school for a few weeks and should have known better than to trust her.

I felt the comb go through my long hair as she asked other girls in the dorm, "What should I do with this country girl's hair?"

I ignored the first comment, thinking she was actually trying to help me fit in, but the combing got more forceful.

"Ow," I said, pulling my hair away.

"Oh, I am sorry, did I hurt you?" she said, pretending to be concerned.

I glared at her. She continued to comb, but even more forcefully this next time, digging the comb into my scalp. I realized at that moment, as two other girls started giggling, that she was doing this on purpose.

"Ouch!" I yelled at her again as she yanked the comb through my hair.

The girl who was combing my hair then hissed in my ear, in Mongolian, "You are a country girl. You are nothing."

I jumped out of my chair, swung around, and hit her so hard that she fell on the ground.

I then ran to the director's office and explained what that girl had done.

"This is not the first time," I said, red in the face with anger. "She always says mean things. I'm done. I am going to leave this school."

The director was upset. He said, "Please don't leave. Let me handle this."

And the next day, that girl apologized.

School got much better after that.

Every so often, Otto would call my dad with an update: "It's coming together!" I could hear his British accent through my dad's cell phone. "I can't wait for you to see it!"

But we soon forgot about the film, my problems adjusting to school, and everything else, when we suffered an unexpected loss in our family. One day in May 2015, as my grandfather was riding his horse, he fell over. It was a heart attack. He died instantly.

We missed my grandfather so much. He was the patriarch. He lived in one of the five gers we erected in the spring and summer pastures. He was the one who taught me how to wrestle. He gave me his blessing to be an eagle hunter. I had just proved to myself that this was my path and had so many questions for him. There was so much more to learn. Without him, it felt lonely.

That summer was such a sad one for my family.

But we continued our life the best we could. I continued to bond with White Feathers and to help my parents with their animals—and to meet tourists, most of whom now wanted to meet the girl who had won the eagle contest. Word was traveling fast, and that summer we had more visitors than ever.

October came quickly, and I entered the Golden Eagle Festival again. This time, I was not the only girl. Two others were competing.

I felt so happy to see them there—and hoped my winning the contest the year before had inspired them each to compete. I was not surprised to see other girls as excited as I had been to be part of this tradition.

That year, I was not as nervous as I had been the

year before, even though I had not spent as much time training White Feathers. She was out of practice, and so was I. I was not concerned, though, as I had already proved myself. It just felt good to be part of the event, part of the tradition.

Otto called that December to say that the film was finished. He wanted us to come to the United States in February 2016 to see it at a film festival called Sundance. That was the first of the many trips I would make to the United States. The second one was to Los Angeles for the Hollywood premiere in October, which meant I had to miss the Golden Eagle Festival that year, but it was worth it. I got to see the movie. I got to see my grandfather again, as he witnessed me winning the Golden Eagle Festival. To see him, so vibrant and alive, was like living in the dream I have had since he died. It was like seeing a ghost.

I must have started trembling because I felt a hand on my shoulder, steadying me.

"It's okay, Aisholpan," my father whispered in my ear.

I turned and saw the blue, silvery light reflecting on his face, like the moonlight does in Mongolia. It lit him up. His big brown eyes were brimming with tears, too, as he said again, "It's okay."

That made me cry even harder.

"You were born to do this," my grandfather told me shortly before he died. "You are Aisholpan, our brightest star. You will show us the way."

I realized, as I sat in that LA theater, that this film was doing more for eagle hunting than I had ever imagined. When the film ended, and I wiped the tears from my face, I felt the applause as much as I heard it. It rumbled up from the floor and throughout my whole body. The entire audience had leaped to their feet; some people were even crying. It reminded me of the crowd's reaction when White Feathers had landed on my arm in five seconds.

Something about my story moved these total strangers to feel all these things.

I stood up and waved, as did my mother and father. And people kept clapping and cheering.

While the film got positive reviews, some people commented that it was not 100 percent accurate. Namely, I learned that I was not the first eagle huntress ever in the world! Just in my family, and the first to have won the Golden Eagle Festival.

My father thought that he was the first man to train his daughter to be an eagle huntress, and that before me there were no eagle huntresses. This was the story both Asher and Otto had believed as well. But we all realized that this wasn't correct when people started writing stories to say, "Aisholpan is not the first!" That was how I learned that eagle huntresses date back as far as 700 BCE. That I was part of a long line of famous eagle huntresses, including Makpal Abdrazakova, an eagle huntress from Kazakhstan who competed in a festival there in 2009, several years before I had won the Golden Eagle Festival.

I am so proud to be among them.

Once the film was out in the world, my life changed even more radically. I became used to flying places and, in the months that followed, went to film festivals and premieres in London, Paris, Athens, Bangkok, Zurich, Beijing, and beyond.

It was wonderful—people were learning about eagle hunting and about our culture. People were mesmerized by the beauty of our land and the purity of our relationship with animals—whether they were Australian, Japanese, or Greek. This story resonated. The film was bigger than me and my story. It was the story of the Kazakh people. It was the story of this remote northwestern corner of Mongolia, where people can still live a nomadic life and hunt with eagles.

FAMOUS IN MONGOLIA—AND BEYOND

My father and I agreed to do the film with Otto because we wanted to share the ancient art of eagle hunting with the world. We had hoped to help revitalize a practice that was threatened with extinction.

It was working.

14

The Aisholpan Effect

I had spent the summer months traveling to so many film festivals and premieres that I did not have time to fly White Feathers or get her ready for the festival. I knew I would be in Ölgii to compete in October 2017, but I also knew that White Feathers was too fat.

When you get your eagle ready to hunt, you have to start thinning her out, making her muscular. You have to train her to keep hunting, rather than feed her like a baby. We had so many tourists visiting us that summer, and they all wanted to meet "the eagle huntress" and her. So, with every fox drag we did for show, she got a piece of meat. Sometimes, if I was not home or available, Saigulikh would go because she looks enough like me. No one complained!

My father was also too busy—between accompanying me to every film premiere and hosting so many tourists, this became his full-time job. Thank goodness my brother had returned from the army. Samrakhan was now living at home with his wife, Alia, and their baby girl, Tansholpan. He took care of all the animals when my dad was away—including my father's eagle and White Feathers.

The Golden Eagle Festival was the first weekend in October, and my father suggested I use his eagle instead of White Feathers. The most important thing in a competition like that, with so many eyes on you, is that your eagle is ready. And we both knew that White Feathers wasn't ready. His eagle was older and more mature. She could handle the crowds and was used to tourists. I would fly her instead.

So much had changed in the two years since I had won the contest. I could tell from the morning I arrived at the festival grounds that it was going to be the biggest event yet. There was a different energy. And so many people! When I competed in 2014, there were six hundred attendees. In 2017, there were more than one thousand.

And this year, there were seven girls competing. Seven!

I saw Zamanbol there, one of the two girls who had competed two years before, and I learned more about her.

"When I was young, my grandfather told me about eagle hunting," she said. "That's how I became one."

She told me that when she saw me compete in 2014, it inspired her to join the competition, too.

THE AISHOLPAN EFFECT

There is a famous Kazakh saying, "From the old horn, which has already grown, it's better to have a new horn, which is growing."

My people say I am the new horn. But I think I am one of many.

ACKNOWLEDGMENTS

From Aisholpan:
While this may be my story, it would not have been possible without the love and support of many people. Thank you to Liz Welch for her friendship and her commitment to helping me tell my story so beautifully; to Farrin Jacobs and the whole team at Little, Brown Books for Young Readers for making this book a reality; to Yerlan Amangeldi, for his dedication to helping me and my family communicate with my publisher; to Rebecca Gradinger, Veronica Goldstein, and Elizabeth Resnick at Fletcher & Company for seeing the potential for a book and guiding me through the process; and to Otto Bell and Stacey Reiss for first sharing my story with the world. I'd also like to thank my father, Nurgaiv "Agilay" Rys, for supporting my

ACKNOWLEDGMENTS

dream to become an eagle huntress; my mother, Alma Koksegen, for believing in me; and White Feathers for being my partner every step of the way.

From Liz:

First off, I would like to thank Aisholpan and her family for trusting me to help her tell her story! For inviting me to sleep in your home, ride your ponies, hold your eagles, and drink salt tea around your table during the magical time I spent in Bayan-Ölgii.

Nurbolat Len, thank you for being such wonderful guide and translator while I was there, and thank you, Yerlan Almankeldi, for keeping me connected when I returned home. I am deeply grateful to you for the hours you spent translating this book word for word—in real time, and at odd hours—with Aisholpan and her family. This book would not exist without your help.

Jeanne Markel, thank you for bringing my attention to *The Eagle Huntress* in the first place. A

ACKNOWLEDGMENTS

special "rakmet" to Chris Wedge. I benefited from your decision to come for your own research. On that note, thank you, Lucy Manos, for your expert itinerary planning!

Rebecca Gradinger, thank you for asking me to help bring this story to the page—and thanks to both Otto Bell and Stacey Reiss for believing that I could. And huge thanks to Veronica Goldstein and Elizabeth Resnick.

Thanks always to my agent Brettne Bloom for letting me focus on the storytelling, and to Farrin Jacobs, one of the most astute, thoughtful, and funniest editors I know.

To my husband, Gideon D'Arcangelo, who did not blink when I said, "So, I am going to Mongolia to live with semi-nomadic eagle hunters for a little while." To my brother, Dan Welch, and my dearest friend, Leslie King, for always being there to help take care of Bella, my daughter.

Last but not least, this book is for Bella, my heart and my reason for writing stories like these.

FURTHER READING

If you're interested in reading more about eagle hunting, Mongolia, or Kazakh culture, here are a few suggestions:

Moving with the Seasons: Portrait of a Mongolian Family by Liza F. Carter (Saltwind Press, 2014)

Horse Song: The Nadaam of Mongolia by Ted and Betsy Lewin (Lee & Low Books, 2008)

Vanishing Cultures: Mongolia by Jan Reynolds (Lee & Low Books, 2007)

KAZAKH GLOSSARY

balakhbau: tethers tied to an eagle's ankles.

baldakh: the leaning stick that an eagle hunter uses to balance the arm that the eagle rests on when the hunter is on horseback. It has a pad on the bottom of the stick that rests on the horse's neck, and then a rope that attaches to the saddle.

berkutchi: an eagle hunter.

besbarmak: a five-fingered meal, or one that is eaten with your hands, that is prepared with goat or lamb or cow, and accompanied by dumplings.

biyalai: the glove made of deer or goat skin worn by eagle hunters to protect his or her skin from being cut by razor-sharp talons.

KAZAKH GLOSSARY

dombra: stringed instrument played by Kazakh nomads.

djem khlata: the sack a hunter carries on hunts that holds food for his or her eagle.

gers: portable, tentlike homes that nomads live in that can be easily erected and disassembled. Made of a collapsible wooden frame, felt lining, cowhide, and plastic sheets.

Huka: the call of an eagle hunter to the eagle.

Jaksi: All right!

Rakmet: Thank you.

saptiayakhk: a wooden bowl used to feed an eagle.

tomaga: the leather hood placed over an eagle's head to keep her calm.

tughir: a wooden perch that the eagle sits on.

DISCUSSION QUESTIONS

1. Aisholpan and her family live a seminomadic lifestyle. How do the seasons change their daily lives? What hardships do the different seasons bring?

2. How do the responsibilities of women and men differ in Aisholpan's culture? How do these differences compare to your culture?

3. Aisholpan relates the story of the white eagle. How does this story reflect the traditions of Aisholpan's family and tribe?

4. The Kazakh people have managed to preserve their way of life despite pressure from other groups. How have external forces changed the Kazakh traditions? In what ways have the Kazakh people succeeded in holding on to those traditions?

5. What is Aisholpan's family's relationship with tourists who come to stay with them? How does each group benefit from the other?

6. Aisholpan's father tells her that "as a hunter, you just want to create the space for your eagle to be

able to do what she does in the wild" (p. 74). How does Aisholpan's tribe view their relationship to animals? How does this compare with your relationship to animals?

7. What rituals do Aisholpan's people have regarding eagle hunting? How does Aisholpan gradually learn to hunt?

8. How does Aisholpan respond to those within her culture who criticize or doubt her ability as an eagle huntress?

9. As a result of the movie about her, Aisholpan travels far away from where she grew up. What differences does she observe between country and city life?

10. When watching the documentary, how does your experience of Aisholpan's story compare to reading the book? What different parts of Aisholpan's story does each medium reveal?

Asher Svidensky

Aisholpan Nurgaiv

is the first female eagle hunter to have competed at the Golden Eagle Festival in Ölgii, Mongolia. Her story was featured in the award-winning documentary film *The Eagle Huntress*. She is currently a high school student in Kazakhstan.

Liz Welch

is an award-winning journalist and memoirist. She is the coauthor of the *New York Times* bestselling *I Will Always Write Back* as well as *The Kids Are All Right*, which won an Alex Award.